Are You Doing Fine, Oklahoma?

Edited by
Catherine L. Hobbs

Mongrel Empire Press
Norman, Oklahoma, USA

FIRST EDITION, 2008
Copyright © 2007 by Catherine L. Hobbs
All rights reserved.

ISBN-13: 978-0-9801684-1-9

A portion of the proceeds from the sale of this collection is donated to the Oklahoma Historical Society.

Cover: "MV-HA-YV (A Person Who Teaches)" by William W. Haney, Jr. Photo by Danielle Knight, 2008.

WWW.MONGRELEMPIREPRESS.COM

Book Design: Mongrel Empire Press using iWork Pages.

This book is dedicated to all our families.

Contents

Prologue:
   Writing About the Oklahoma Centennial — i

Part I: Popular Histories of Oklahoma Origins

1. Blood, Sweat, and Tears:
   The Creation of Oklahoma's Black Towns — 1
2. The Creek Nation in Oklahoma — 17
3. Marry an Agrarian and Knit Your Stockings Red, or, How Oklahoma Socialists Rethought the Family Farm — 37
4. The Territory of Terror:
   The Outlaws and Lawmen of Oklahoma — 55

Part II: Reflecting on Identity in Oklahoma

5. I Don't Know if I Belong to the Land — 83
6. The Story Beneath the Glare — 91
7. My Way to Rainy Mountain — 99

Part III: Shared & Sharing—Experiencing Oklahoma and the Centennial

8. Oklahoma Centennial Bowie Knife — 107
9. A Day of Mixed Feelings — 111
10. Sweet Treats and Good Eats:
    A Look at Oklahoma's Unique Restaurants — 123
11. Caught Up in Celebration:
    Remembering the Oklahoma Centennial Parade — 135
12. This is Oklahoma Football… — 141

Epilogue:
   Are You Doing Fine, Oklahoma?
         An Assessment at 100 Years — 149

Contributors — 153

Are You Doing Fine, Oklahoma?

Prologue: Writing About the Oklahoma Centennial
by Catherine L. Hobbs

This collection of essays and articles about the Oklahoma centennial contains writing by students in a special advanced composition class fall 2007 at the University of Oklahoma. The OU English department's writing track has offered a course on writing about Oklahoma for more than a decade, most often taught by my friend and OU colleague Prof. Susan Kates. Kates came to Oklahoma from Columbus, Ohio, in 1995 and with her love of the prairies immediately "went native." She began the class in 2002 not long after Oklahoma writer Rilla Askew held a special seminar on "writing from your Oklahoma roots" in 1997 for the Oklahoma Scholar-Leadership Enrichment program (OSLEP). Askew has been around the English department in one capacity or another since then, early on teaching the class herself or lately making an appearance in Prof. Kates's class Reading and Writing Oklahoma: Region and Representation.

Nevertheless, even though I was a native Oklahoman, I had never taught the class myself. Suddenly, it was my turn in fall 2007, and it was the state's centennial!

Over summer 2007, I hastily prepared, going so far as to fashion an authentic 1907 college faculty costume, navy blue gored skirt and a high-collared white blouse. I decided that the new <u>Historical Atlas of Oklahoma</u> would make a fine anchor for the course, helping orient students to the state's history while providing them with hundreds of ideas for articles. Of course, we also had other readings in general history and culture from the period. The genre of popular or journalistic history seemed appropriate for students to focus on for the written pieces, rather than history proper. Students would also write memoir and personal essays as they did in other advanced writing courses.

Starting with 15 highly motivated and talented students, (ending with about a dozen), the class began by writing the four longer collaborative essays you see here in section one. Each group chose its own topic after a period in which the class read and discussed historical material including the <u>Atlas</u>. The more personal essays and memoirs came near the end of the fall semester after students had gotten to know each other better and reflected more on their relationships with the state. We also enjoyed special guests for the class, including Professor Dorscine Spigner Littles, human relations, who brought a video she had made on early African-American women in Oklahoma, and the English Department's Professor Catherine John, who shared in a discussion of the video.

Everyone in class also attended one or more centennial events, and during the centennial week, we offered our own program of celebration—for the centennial, naturally, but perhaps as well for the easing up of labor on research and writing projects! Students planned a spirited, fun, and significant centennial event. Our program was full of student-made music, readings, Oklahoma trivia contests and awards, along with some critique of the state's attitudes and problems.

Now we publicly offer a portion of this semester's work to commemorate not only the centennial, but also our busy and intense time of learning about and reflecting on the state's beginnings as well as remembering and reflecting on our own relationships with Oklahoma. As we were researching the photographs to include with this collection, we discovered a collection of Oklahoma Golden Jubilee essays in the archives of the Oklahoma Historical Society. They are described as "Essays Written By Students For The Semi-centennial. Topics Include The Green Corn Rebellion, John B. Doolin, Halliburton, Etc." with "Caeser Bruner" and "Robert S. Kerr" listed as the "Creator" of the collection. We are happy to recognize our predecessors and hope to honor the tradition with our contribution.

Oklahoma poet Jeanetta Calhoun Mish taught one of our class sessions and participated in other ways, becoming our greatest supporter and cheerleader. The class came to believe its own hypothesis, that we were sisters. ("Get a hat like your sister's," they demanded one day when she came in wearing a beret.) So Jeanetta became "my sister," and I am proud to claim her.

I thank Jeanetta especially for offering to publish our work through Mongrel Empire Press, the publishing house established by her and her husband, OU Engineering professor, Kyran Mish. She announced her offer to publish just as applause for our centennial program died down that cold and blustery November day. We both knew the book would serve as a golden cord knotting up the memory of all our centennial rememberings.

Part 1
Popular Histories of Oklahoma Origins

1. Blood, Sweat, and Tears: The Creation of Oklahoma's Black Towns
By Sarah Buchanan, Elisabeth Brown, and Gage Jeter

Beulah, or heaven, they were promised—a romantic land of beauty with open skies surrounding rolling hills, and plains that stretched further than imagination would allow. They imagined a peaceful prairie breeze would sway the trees as they set up camp. Yet along the way they came to realize that at the end of this trail lay not the promised land, but a frontier of tears and trials of spirit.

They arrived to find the harshest weather in the world. Hot tornadic winds scoured the Earth in summer and the brittle brown grass snapped when a foot crushed it. With winter came the threat of blizzards, and early spring froze tender crops. This land followed the sun to the sky in moments of quiet, and at times its loneliness was interrupted by a violent thunderclap and wild weather. But always, there was the wind.

Yet it was here, in Indian Territory, that the former slaves found their solace, for a brief moment.

Although most blacks came to Oklahoma to acquire their "promised land," others, black slaves of Native American tribes, were forced to move. Like their owners, the slaves moved on trails, or "forced marches," such as the 1838 Cherokee relocation called the Trail of Tears. The migration from several Southern states across the nation was tough for the slaves, the terrain was hard, and the journey long. They fought for their lives along the way. It took all the strength they had to keep moving as they

I. Popular Histories of Oklahoma Origins

endured harsh weather conditions and the threat of disease.

As historian Linda Reese describes in Freedmen: "Black slaves performed much of the physical labor involved in removal. For example, they loaded wagons, cleared the roads, and led the teams of livestock along the way." Many, like their owners, lost their lives on these trips. But for those who made it to Indian Territory, their final camp was often not much better than the trail.

The Cherokee Nation was the first to free their slaves, doing so in June 1863. Although these freed slaves were treated differently depending on the tribe they associated with, their rights were often limited. Although segregation laws, called Jim Crow, did not come about until after Oklahoma's statehood, segregation and white supremacy was part of Southern ideology at the time. This ideology kept African Americans from participating in the same communal activities as their white and Native American neighbors. Jim Crow practices and later laws only gave the poorly treated blacks more reason to fight for their ultimate equality.

Although most African Americans weren't freed until after the Civil War, many black soldiers fought alongside their white comrades in battle. One of the key battles in which black soldiers fought alongside white and Native Americans was the Battle of Honey Springs, on July 17, 1863. This battle was a significant victory for the Union because it ended the war in the present territory of the state and strengthened the Union's efforts to gain control of Indian Territory. Black troops proved themselves worthy soldiers and built forts in Oklahoma to fight bandits and other outlaws and policed borders during land runs. They gained the respect of Native Americans in the Indian Wars of 1873, earning the nickname "Buffalo Soldiers" for their troops' work during peacetime.

After the Civil War, the U.S. government abolished slavery. Along with this, the new freedmen and black settlers of Oklahoma gained the right to vote, and former slaves of the Five Nations assimilated into their respective tribal groups with full citizenship rights. At first the Five Nations were hesitant—they didn't want to give the former slaves political power, tribal money, and access to the land, but they were willing to end slavery. Negotiations with the government were drawn out, but eventually each of the five tribes agreed to the terms, allowing the freed slaves their rights and citizenship.

After the War the newly freed Southern slaves wanted a new beginning, a chance to start a new way of life. All ideas and dreams were directed to one place: Oklahoma. According to historian Gates, Oklahoma was frequently called "The Promised Land." Many blacks heard it advertised as "heaven on earth." After seeing and hearing the advertisements about the economic success and promise that Oklahoma held, many packed up their households and began the trek to this newly settled territory. As historian Mozell C. Hill writes, this migration to Oklahoma was a "racial movement in which Negroes attempted to 'escape' the social pressure of the dominant white culture." The unknown of the West was much more promising than the white supremacy and tyranny of the South.

Living in the South with little to no money, many former slaves had to sell most of their belongings before heading West. Traveling conditions were poor. Food and decent shelter were lacking. What

I. Popular Histories of Oklahoma Origins

possessions they kept were piled into the backs of wagons. Sadly, this meant that many children's toys were left in the South. Historian Gates explains, "Using meager means, mothers used string and yarn to make small 'prairie string dolls' for them to play with on the way to Oklahoma."

For many, the move was tough. The dirt roads were rough and crowded. With little to no room in the wagon trains for belongings, much less people, most travelers walked or came by wagon train from states like Georgia, Louisiana, and Mississippi. They had very little money, poor food and clothing, and they were carrying as many possessions as possible. These problems were nothing in light of the new world they faced when they arrived in Oklahoma, full of new chances and new freedoms. When they finally arrived in Oklahoma, the paradise they expected did not exist, at least at the beginning. The dusty, dirt roads had brought them to Oklahoma with no finances, modest education to start with, and only plans of doing farmwork. But that did not discourage many of these new settlers.

One former slave found himself inspired by religion and helped form some of Oklahoma's new churches. In his autobiography in the collected WPA Slave Narratives of Oklahoma, the Rev. William L. Bethel recounts his experiences as an African American man in Oklahoma territory.

Reverend Bethel was born a slave on May 4, 1844, in Clemmonsville, North Carolina. His master and mistress's names were Josiah and Eliza Bethel. Reverend Bethel says, "I was quite a pet of the mistress, and every morning and night my master would put his hand on my head and pray." Josiah Bethel was a Methodist preacher, and while William

Bethel was a young slave, his master's family moved often. They moved to Greensboro, where William spent his childhood and lived until the Civil War.

At about 18 years old, Reverend Bethel went to Bristow, Virginia, and enlisted in the Army. He explains that he then went to Richmond, where he worked on "breastworks" (fortifications). "One of our favorite songs was: 'Look over in the Valley, don't you see it lighten, looks like we are going to have a storm, but altho you are mistaken, 'tis the darky soldiers' buttons shining on the uniform.' After surrender we went to Raleigh, North Carolina, where we were mustered out."

In 1872 he married Mrs. Fannie Elizabeth Martin and purchased a home in Raleigh and one acre of land. He then built a frame cabin, where their first child, Carrie Lee Bethel, was born. The next year, 1873, William entered Lincoln University, in Chester County, Pennsylvania. He worked for his board with Dr. Golder, who was then the President of Livingston College, in Saul's Borough, North Carolina. "I was graduated from Lincoln University in the year 1882. In the same year on the 12th day of April, 1882, I was licensed to preach," he wrote.

Slave owners taught Christianity to many slaves in the South, although in many states, slaves were legally forbidden to read and write. Historian William Courtland Johnson writes: "Nearly all interpretations of slave religion maintained that… Southern planters motivated by… sincere concern for the salvation of bondsmen… introduced Christianity to the spiritually starved slave community." This conversion to Christianity began before the start of the Civil War. Many of the blacks who fought in the war sang hymns and spiritual

I. Popular Histories of Oklahoma Origins

poetry to get them through the rough nights, just as they had sung in the fields. Not all plantation owners wanted their slaves to receive an education, much less learn about Christianity. Others were indifferent to the religious education of their slaves (Johnson, 298).

Historian Albert J. Raboteau argues, "Not all slaves were Christian... [But] the doctrines, symbols, and vision of life preached by Christianity were familiar to most." Many slaves were unable or refused to join churches, yet they still acknowledged Christian beliefs. As Johnson reports, evangelists from the North described, "appalling state of 'religious disrepair,' particularly in the newly settled Southwest." Once freed and beginning to settle in Oklahoma, more opportunity for believers to come together was found through the church. Some who were believers, like William Bethel, found an opportunity to succeed economically in this new territory through preaching and organizing.

Shortly after, in 1884, William Bethel's wife died. He then moved to Winston Salem, organized a Presbyterian Church, and then served a church at Sanford, North Carolina. He returned to Winston Salem, North Carolina and married his second wife, Nannie L. Brown. In 1901, the couple moved to Oklahoma Territory. "The first place I lived after reaching Oklahoma Territory was Kingfisher. We then moved to Anadarko, where I purchased a home and organized a Presbyterian Church and Sunday School, and also organized churches all over the Oklahoma Territory."

They moved to Oklahoma City in 1904 and again purchased land. Bethel also organized a church in Oklahoma City where he received three Enabling

Acts in 1907. An enabling act is a piece of legislation that authorizes a person or group to take certain actions, in this case to organize Presbyterian churches. Bethel was also honored because while he was at the denomination's General Assembly, [in] Des Moines, Iowa, "I was called on to give the Benediction."

Not all black slaves who came from the South looking for success found it. As the Federal Writers collection reports, Alice Alexander, born in 1839, came from Louisiana to Oklahoma, walking "nally all the way." The travels were long, taking anywhere from three to six months, depending on where the settlers came from and how they traveled. Alice left Louisiana, "came in soch of ejecation... we come to Oklahoma looking for de same than then dat darkies go north looking fer now. We got dissipinted." Some blacks were able to settle down in communities and start education classes for the younger groups. Others immediately began working on farms, using what knowledge they had from working on plantations.

After managing, working, and living on plantations for so long, pioneers knew how to establish themselves on the land with few resources. Gates states that "they lived in hastily thrown together shelters; they ate what they could trap and forage." Settling in Oklahoma was a continuation of their struggles, but they succeeded and worked to persevere through the worst of it. Communities began to be formed, especially in the Tulsa region, where stories, ideas, and hopes of economic success filtered through the ears of African-American farmers and workers. Neighbors learned from each

I. Popular Histories of Oklahoma Origins

other and exchanged ideas on how to breed success from nature's resources.

While African Americans in Oklahoma led harsh lives, they developed a strong sense of community with a rich variety of cultural traditions. Bound by their shared hardships and joys, African Americans intertwined music performances, religious customs and oral traditions in their daily lives. Each of these elements helped to provide them with a sense of cohesion and pride in their culture.

Children were told West African folk tales, or wise and entertaining "trickster tales." These animal-related stories consistently showed one weak character outsmarting a stronger one that was trying to control or overpower them. These stories helped raise the morale of formerly oppressed slaves.

African American culture centered on music. Used not only as a celebration of their heritage, musical traditions created a stronger sense of themselves as a people. Some of these lyrical songs, known as sorrow songs or spirituals, were first used as the slaves' way of expression, prayer or protest. They also incorporated instruments such as drums, horns and fiddles into their singing. Dance became another means of expression; dancers incorporated meaningful movement with the songs. This strong bond of their heritage and traditions began within the community.

Many African American "promoters" wanted to "spur black colonization of both Oklahoma Territory and Indian Territory." However, as time went on, others wished to persecute blacks as they were being maltreated in the South. In 1892, a group of white men ran blacks out of the town of Lexington, an established black settlement in Oklahoma. Another instance was in the town of Blackwell in 1893. African Americans were chased out of town by white terrorists.

When some African Americans held their claim and would not leave the state, whites decided to punish them even further—through education. In 1897, the Oklahoma Territorial Legislature forbade racial mixing in classrooms and schoolhouses. This was the beginning of segregation that African Americans thought they had escaped.

Permanent housing and communities soon were available for more settlers. As historian Hill writes, they had settled into "'Boom Towns,' established as a result of… rushes for gold, land, oil, and other natural wealth offered on the frontier." They began picking up small, odd jobs, working for whatever pay they could get. Shelters soon turned into farms and houses. While blacks still lived in intense poverty, they used their knowledge from their lives in the South and applied it to the new living establishments. As Gates notes, "They knew which side of land to build the house on… to locate their barns far enough from the house…" so as to help their new way of life thrive. The black Southerners did not need formal education to prove that they could accomplish something in this new territory.

As a result of population growth and also segregation and terrorism by white supremacists, all-black towns in Oklahoma began to be formed. Some African-Americans felt the only way to escape the persecution they faced was to live in an all-black town. Each town has an interesting history that exemplifies the African-American culture and perseverance.

I. Popular Histories of Oklahoma Origins

The formation, location, success, and failures of all-black towns in Oklahoma varies, as seen with major all-black towns including Langston, Red Bird, and Boley. All three were formed around the same time period, from 1890 to 1903, but were formed on different grounds and for different reasons. Today, all three are still standing – some more solidly than others – but nevertheless the history vividly remains.

Langston, established on October 22, 1890, was founded by E.P. McCabe in order to encourage the formation of all-black towns in hopes for an all-black state of Oklahoma. In McCabe's own words, "Langston City is a Negro city, and we are proud of the fact. Her city officers are all colored. Her teachers are colored." McCabe's goal was simple: he wished to reach out to other blacks by portraying Langston as the most ideal place to live in order to achieve a notable population center. His goal was met, and all expectations were exceeded as Langston was formed and began to take a unique shape of its own.

Located near present day Guthrie, Langston is named after John Mercer Langston, a well known public figure and black leader during this early period. Langston drew in many blacks because the area was touted as the "land of milk and honey." This advertisement brought in people by the hundreds, resulting in growth of not only population, but of economics as well. By 1892, approximately twenty-five businesses were serving the community of Langston. With over 600 citizens and numerous businesses quickly springing up, Langston was on target to be a first-rate example of a successful black town.

The milk and honey did not last for long however. Around 1943 the population began to drop for many reasons. Poverty was high, businesses were not having much success, and the town's government was unstable. Also, the college students attending Langston University were not on the best of terms with the other community people, and there was a constant struggle between town and gown.

Described as Langston's "crown jewel," Langston University is an active college today that had its share of difficult times during those early years. Established in 1897, the "Colored Agricultural and Normal University" was established as a teacher's college and strived to "instruct both male and female Colored persons in the art of teaching various branches with pertain to a common school education and in such higher education as may be deemed advisable..."

The second example, the town of Red Bird, located in present day Wagoner County and well known for its historic landmarks, was officially established in 1902. E.L. Barber is said to have founded the town, with stories telling that its name came from all the red birds that flocked around the area. Others from around the U.S. took notice of this town, such as two Arkansas travelers, H.E. Frith and R.C. Waltoc. "We spent a day at Red Bird and found the location much better than it is advertised...We can say this is the best town in this country...for the Negro who wants to make money and get a home that will be a credit to himself and family." With people like Mr. Frith and Mr. Waltoc, the word was being spread that Red Bird was the place to be, and others took notice.

Red Bird's peak years occurred around 1920, when the town's population was at its highest, at approximately 400 citizens. The 1920s also marked the decade where the issue of keeping blacks from

I. Popular Histories of Oklahoma Origins

voting centered around the town and its people. L.E. Barber, the son of E.L. Barber, organized a political campaign to overturn an Oklahoma constitutional amendment calling for the disfranchisement of blacks. This bold move eventually failed, but the campaign was a bonding tool for the community.

Other significant aspects of Red Bird today are its historical landmarks. Miller-Washington School, one of the most important buildings in Red Bird, has been named to the list of the National Register of Historic Places. Included also in this elite list is the Red Bird City Hall, known as "The Court House." Recognized on the state level, the Oklahoma Landmarks Inventory includes the Red Bird Drug Store and Red Bird City Jail as distinguished historical facilities.

While the town itself may not be thriving as it once was, these landmarks still represent what once was, and what will always be the spirit of Red Bird. Buildings, a water tower, and a church still exist throughout the small town, and the sign proclaiming "Welcome to Red Bird" continues to greet all who enter.

Boley's roots come from a story, in which two men challenged each other as to whether or not a black town could be formed and successfully run by blacks. One man said yes, the other said no, and so the bet was on. Officially credited with forming the town of Boley was Thomas N. Haynes. Haynes came to Boley in 1905 and organized a petition asking for the formation of the town. The federal court in Sapulpa passed the petition and the town of Boley was created. The town wasted no time, elections were held, and Haynes became the first mayor of Boley.

1. Blood, Sweat & Tears

Boley began as a small, quaint town near central Oklahoma in 1905, but by 1911 the population had grown to nearly 7,000. This dramatic change in population made the once small town in Oklahoma the biggest all-black towns in the country, and its rapid growth was recognized across the nation. This successful "experiment" resulted in the formation of one of the most successful all-black towns in history.

Uncle Jesse, the town poet, might have said it best when he wrote "Oh, 'tis a pretty country and the Negroes own it too, With not a single white man here, To tell us what to do – in Boley." The rapid growth of the town is invisible to us today, but the existence of numerous businesses, stores, restaurants, and offices speak for themselves. The blacks had succeeded in forming and successfully managing and maintaining a town without any help from whites. Lake Moore, the white supremacist who argued that blacks could not successfully set up, run, and maintain their own community lost the bet. Boley thrived, and it was proven that blacks could indeed take care of themselves.

The hard-beaten red dirt of Oklahoma, began with the many diverse settlers who walked this land before us. They, too, gazed at the orange and pink horizon; their eyes held a hope of what could be, and of what was to come. While Langston, Boley, and Red Bird are just a few of the towns that these strong African Americans established in the state, they stand for more than just a "black community." These towns stand for perseverance, dignity, survival, and fortitude. The narratives and tales that surround the formation of the black settlements are what keep their spirit alive in Oklahoma today.

I. Popular Histories of Oklahoma Origins

This article is drawn from and refers to the following sources:

Reese, Linda. Oklahoma's Historical Society's Encyclopedia of Oklahoma History and Culture, "Freedmen," 2003 <http://digital.library.okstate.edu/encyclopedia/entries/F/FR016.html>; Tipton, Bertha P., Interviewer. "Alice Alexander Interview." The New Deal Network.; Baker T. Lindsay and Julie P. Baker, ed. The WPA Oklahoma Slave Narratives. Norman: University of Oklahoma Press, 1996; Johnson, Hannibal B. Acres of Aspiration: The All-Black Towns of Oklahoma; Hill, Mozell C. "The All-Negro Communities of Oklahoma: The Natural History of a Social Movement: Part I"; Taylor, Quintard. "African American Men in the American West, 1528-1990"; "African Americans, Oklahoma's History. <www.state.ok.us/osfdocs/stinfo2.html>; "African Americans." Oklahoma History: A StudentGuide. <www.otrd.state.ok.us/StudentGuide/history.html>; Oklahoma Historical Society's Encyclopedia of Oklahoma History & Culture. <http://digital.library.okstate.edu/encyclopedia/entries/F/FR016.html>; BuffaloSoldiers.com; The African-American Registry. "September 22: Boley, OK." <http://www.aaregistry.com/african_american_history/2054/Boley_Oklahoma_a_FUBU_of_towns>; Thomas, John D. "Oklahoma Towns Born of Struggle and Hope." New York Times. 02/08/2004./

1. Blood, Sweat & Tears

Boley, Oklahoma - "Farmers and Merchants Bank" - David J. Turner on steps. 1860s -Courtesy of the Oklahoma Historical Society. Towns Collection #3377-B-1.

I. Popular Histories of Oklahoma Origins

Boley, Oklahoma "Members of the Town Council" - L. to R. Front: 1. 2. 3. David J. Turner, banker 4. Thomas Hayner, Boley Promoter. 1860s. Courtesy of the Oklahoma Historical Society. Towns Collection #3377-D-1

2. The Creek Nation in Oklahoma
By Sydney Teel &
Andrew Edgren

The 19th century was the most turbulent period of Creek history. Because of events in the 19th century, Creeks today no longer have complete tribal autonomy. The Nation is no longer a political unit that lives only according to its own rules. It is now a part of the American public, and individual Creeks must now find a place within American society. Full tribal autonomy officially ended in the late 19th century, but the events throughout the entire century foreshadowed and initiated this loss. The continual loss of land, due to treaties and laws created by the United States, endured until the Creek Nation not only lost all of its original homeland in what is now Alabama and Georgia, but also lost its new homeland in what is now Oklahoma. Forced assimilation, through the arrival of missions, schools, and commerce in Indian Territory, also accompanied the loss of land. This change ended up further dividing the Creek Nation, which already had a history of disunity and disagreement between tribal members. The history of the Creek Nation during the 19th century is one of continual loss in key aspects of the community.

Creek Life in Alabama/Georgia and the Removal to Indian Territory

In her article about the removal of the Five Nations tribes, historian Mary Young discusses the unfairness of the treatment and forced removal of the Southeastern tribes. Referring to President Andrew Jackson, she writes, "The President's

I. Popular Histories of Oklahoma Origins

justification of Indian removal was the one usually applied to the displacement of the Indians by newer Americans – the superiority of a farming to a hunting culture, and of Anglo-American 'liberty, civilization, and religion' to the strange and barbarous way of the red man." The Creeks were considered one of the Five "Civilized" Tribes because they had fairly good relations with whites and their communities were already based upon agriculture. Yet, they were removed from their homelands in Alabama and Georgia to Indian Territory in the 1830s. Their removal was based more upon the desires of white Americans to own the Creek lands, rather than the justification put forth by President Jackson.

Traditionally, the Creek Nation had divisions within its tribe for much of its early history. Historian Michael Green identifies the two different strands of the Creek Tribe. One group of towns, known as "white towns," focused on peacetime interests, while the other, "red towns," centered on wartime interests. Rivalries and differences between these groups, reflected in activities such as athletic competitions, were present for several centuries. Over time, as trading with European colonists progressed, the Creeks kept a distinction between their towns, but began to consider the differences in geography as more of an effect on a town's identity than the traditional red/white division. Therefore, towns in the Chattahoochee Valley, which was "between the present cities of Columbus, Georgia and Eufaula, Alabama," came to be called the "Lower Towns," while the towns lying along the Coosa, Tallapoosa, and Alabama Rivers were known as the "Upper Towns."

As Europeans continued to interact and trade with the Creeks, the differences in the towns became more and more noticeable because the Lower Creeks were geographically closer to Europeans, while the Upper Creeks were geographically secluded. The differences that evolved from these distinctions aided the factionalism and conflict within the Creek Nation during the early 19th century, when the United States desired the Creek lands and wanted the Creeks to either assimilate or move out west.

Inside all of the Five Nations tribes, factionalism erupted between those who were less progressive and those who were more progressive. Young writes that full-blood Indians were more traditional, while Indians with white relatives and mixed-blood Indians became more assimilated into American society through their proximity to settlers and therefore were more willing to give up their old lifestyles. These two factions clashed over issues, such as the cession of their lands and the incorporation of their culture into American society. The two mindsets were especially polarized in Creek society because of the clear differences between the more traditional Creeks of the Upper Towns and the more progressive Creeks of the Lower Towns.

The conflict that arose during and after the 1925 "Treaty of Indian Springs" was an example of this factionalism. Green writes about the trouble surrounding the treaty. While the Creek Council, which incorporated both Lower and Upper tribal leaders, took a strong traditionalist stance against giving land to the American government, some Lower Creeks disobeyed tribal law and tried to sell a large portion of their tribe's land in exchange for individual bribes from the United States. On

I. Popular Histories of Oklahoma Origins

February 12, 1825, a few Lower Creek Indians, led by William McIntosh, signed the treaty, which sold a large portion of Creek land, mostly from the Lower Towns but also including some from the Upper Creek country. Although McIntosh and the other treaty signers did not have the authority to cede the land, as the Creek council had already ruled against signing the treaty, the United States government accepted their signatures anyway. Creek leaders executed McIntosh and some of the other treaty-signers, and the Creek Council argued that the treaty was invalid. The government still ratified it, though.

Green writes that in the next year, Creeks agreed to sign a new treaty, the "Treaty of Washington," with the United States in order to nullify the "Treaty of Indian Springs." This new treaty, however, still ceded the Georgia land to the United States and gave special privileges to those Creeks who moved to Indian Territory. The Historical Atlas of Oklahoma says that the Creeks who first moved to Indian Territory at this time were primarily Lower Town Creeks, especially those with ties to William McIntosh.

By 1832, the Creeks, realizing that the United States would eventually force them to sell their lands, decided to make the best possible negotiation with the government. Main provisions of the "Treaty of 1832" included Creeks giving all of their land on the eastern side of the Mississippi River to the government, but the United States allowing individuals to own separate allotments of land; the government's removing all intruders from these allotments, and the United States giving provisions and unclaimed land in the West, which would be under tribal government, to those Creeks who moved to Indian Territory. Despite the promises of the United States in the treaty, the agreements made were not kept.

First, as Young discusses in her article, white settlers who bought Native American lands took advantage of the Indians selling their allotted territory because those Indians did not understand the value of their land in the United States' economy. White Americans had no problem enticing the Creeks, and other Five Nations Indians, to sell their land for much less value than was fair.

Creeks also had to deal with intense intrusion upon their lands. According to Green, the United States did not keep white settlers from interfering with Creek lands, even after signing the "Treaty of 1832," whose Article Five promised the government's protection from settlers. Because both the state government and federal government refused to protect Creek lands from intruders, Creeks and settlers fought with each other. In turn, this fighting gave the United States a reason to forcibly remove the Creeks to the Indian Territory west of the Mississippi River, even though the conflict between Creeks and other settlers was a direct result of the government's own inability to follow its agreement in the "Treaty of 1832." In 1836, the United States began forcing the Creeks in the Southeast to move to Indian Territory.

Young observes that, in the end, the allotment treaties were actually an "attempt to apply Anglo-American notions of justice, which enshrined private property in land and freedom of contract as virtually absolute values, to Indian tribes whose tastes and traditions were otherwise." The Creeks had a different perspective on property and an ideal society than the traditional Euro-American perspective. Of course, this idea of property and culture did not help the Creeks, who were forced to give up not only their tribal homeland in the Southeast, but also, by the end of the 19th century, to give up their tribal lands in what is now the state of Oklahoma.

Creek Life in Indian Territory

Article 14 of the "Treaty of 1832," the stated, "The Creek country west of the Mississippi shall be solemnly guarantied to the Creek Indians, nor shall any State or Territory ever have a right to pass laws for the government of such Indians, but they shall be allowed to govern themselves." However, over the decades between removal to Indian Territory and Oklahoma statehood, the United States government disregarded this statement and continuously tried to influence the Creeks and impose rules upon the tribe. The government initiated treaties and laws that ceded land, promoted white intrusion and commerce with the building of railroads through Creek lands, and ultimately forced the Creek Nation to break up its tribal lands for good.

According to historian Douglas Hurt, immediately following the removal, the Creek Nation kept more of its original culture than many of the other Indian tribes that were removed from their homelands to Indian Territory. They continued many of their old customs, including naming their towns to match the original ones in the Southeast and keeping the same town political structure, which was based on the old divisions between Upper and Lower Towns. The full traditional schedule of Creek ceremonies and festivals survived the move intact, although the level of observance varied between the two different kinds of towns. Many Upper Creeks held onto their traditions and, therefore, attempted to isolate their towns from government interference in order to maintain their traditional religious and social structures. Instead of valuing old customs, many of the Lower Creeks focused on succeeding in farming and the American economy. These differences had developed between the towns before the forced removal to Indian Territory, but strengthened in the United States' continuing attempts to assimilate Indian tribes into American ways of life.

In spite of these differences between towns, or rather because of the strong differences, United States officials pressed the two sections of Creek towns to come together in a National Council in 1839. Hurt argues that the government's interest in uniting the Creeks stemmed from the desire to influence a single group of leaders rather than the many leaders of the divided Creek towns. The Creek Agent, who represented the United States' wishes, helped to prop up the less traditional Lower Town leaders, at a numerical disadvantage in the meetings, against the Upper Creek leaders, who usually dominated the National Council politics because of their larger numbers. This fighting continued until after the Civil War. To help control the territory after the war, the U.S. government forced the two sections of Creeks to create a single constitution. (See "Civil War" below for more history of Creeks in the war.)

The Creeks, as a whole, did not easily accept Christianity, especially because the traditional, conservative Upper Towns outnumbered the more assimilated Lower Towns. Hurt notes that although three Christian churches existed in Creek territory in 1836, the tribal leaders initially discouraged their members from participating in the religion. For

I. Popular Histories of Oklahoma Origins

example, the Creeks banned missionaries until 1842. However, in exchange for teachers moving to the area, the Creeks revoked the ban. Missionaries succeeded in converting some Creeks, especially in the Lower Towns, and by the 1850s, a large portion of both Upper and Lower Creeks participated in Christianity.

Missionaries first attempted to convert tribal leaders, hoping this would then trickle down to the other tribal members. Although some Creeks replaced their old religious customs with Christianity, especially in the Lower Towns, the conversion of Creeks did not lead to the destruction of their native culture altogether. Hurt writes that many of the more traditional Upper Creek congregations bridged the new religion with their old social and religious customs. For instance, they sang hymns in their native language and celebrated both Christian and Creek festivals. Nevertheless, some traditional Creek towns disagreed with missionary intrusion and occasionally reacted to their presence by ransacking churches and attacking the missionaries.

Even after they converted, Upper Creek and Lower Creek differences exerted themselves in their choices of denomination. Many Lower Creeks favored Methodist and Presbyterian denominations, which allowed these Creeks to continue to supplant their old communal religious customs with the more individual, Americanized ways of worship. The Upper Creeks preferred Baptist churches, which were more locally governed and congregational, allowing Creeks to keep their collective social traditions more intact.

The construction of schools, both day and boarding, followed the arrival of missionaries. Although the Creeks wanted their children to be educated, the lessons that white teachers prepared for their new pupils were restrictive. Hurt says that most schools heavily emphasized learning the English language and rejecting traditional Creek values, which resulted in punishment for those Creek children who spoke their own language or followed their old customs. In addition, Creek children learned to follow traditional American gender roles.

White educators realized that boarding schools allowed teachers to fully indoctrinate Creek children with white values, and five were eventually constructed in the Creek nation. In these schools, children were completely separated from their families and fully immersed in American ways of life. One of the most famous of these was the Presbyterian Tullahassee Mission, which operated from 1850 to 1907. It was set in Wagoner County, near assimilated Creek communities and away from the more traditional tribal areas. Its success led to the Methodist church opening the Asbury Manual Labor School, another boarding school with a similar intent.

As far as creating a new generation of Creeks who could function in mainstream white society, these new schools failed. Hurt discusses the difficulty of American-educated Creeks in Indian Territory. Creeks who attended these schools and performed well found themselves ostracized in their old towns. In addition, when they attempted to enter the general American population, they did not fit in because of their Indian heritage. This rejection left them unable to find a definite place in either society. After the 1850s, the increase of Christianity and the

I. Popular Histories of Oklahoma Origins

English language in the area helped to make attendance at these schools more acceptable. The schools were usually connected strongly to missionaries though, and the majority of traditional Creeks continued to reject other white institutions that attempted to force them into American culture.

Despite the fact that they were no longer living on their native land and outside forces constantly intruded upon them, the traditional Creek worldview still connected the land to its concept of people and spirituality. Because of this traditional mindset, Creeks began to feel a deep affinity for their new home in Indian Territory. Hurt writes that Creek notions of the home, family, and sacred tradition were closely tied to their natural surroundings. Many Creeks even began to adopt new sacred sites to replace the ones they had lost and create new cultural myths incorporating their new homeland. For example, Louis Oliver wrote a poem entitled "The Sharpbreasted Snake," in which he described a snake monster that traverses through the new Creek lands in Oklahoma. He described some of the movements.

> Come to rest by
> Tuskeegi Town, buried
> its self in a lake of
> mud to rest. The
> warriors of Tustanuggi
> were ordered to shoot
> it with a silver tipped
> arrow. With a great
> roar and upheaval The
> Snake moved on;
> winding by Okmulgee
> To enter (Okta hutcher)
> South Canadian River.

The relationship with the land was so closely related to Creek spirituality and life that Creeks began to create the same kinds of stories that tied myth to the earth in their new homeland as they did in their original homeland.

The Civil War and its Aftermath

Although the Civil War was a conflict between the United States and the seceded states of the Confederacy, Indian Territory tribal members experienced a much fighting within their individual tribes. In their article "Red vs. Black: Conflict and Accommodation in the Post Civil War Indian Territory," Historians Donald A. Grinde, Jr. and Quintard Taylor described the fighting within Indian Territory tribes and the pressures they felt from the two sides. The Nations in Indian Territory felt increasing pressure to join the Confederacy throughout the war. The Union took its troops out of the area, leaving the territory open to the Confederacy, while many of the federally appointed Indian agents in the territory sided with the South. Also, the Confederacy promised the tribes more favorable treaties than those created by the Union. As a result of these pressures, all five "Civilized" Tribes, including the Creek, had signed treaties with the South by the end of 1861.

When hostilities began, the United States withdrew its federal troops, who were sent to the Creek Nation to maintain order, so that they could participate in the heavier fighting in the East. Hurt notes that in the absence of Union soldiers, the Confederate Commissioner to Indian Territory, Albert Pike, began to approach Creek leaders about an alliance. His goal was to negotiate a deal that would prevent Union troops from using Indian

I. Popular Histories of Oklahoma Origins

Territory as a hub for its military and keep the area between Texas and Arkansas in the hands of the Confederacy. Unfortunately, Pike underestimated the deep ideological differences between the different groups of Creeks.

Not all of the Native Americans in Indian Territory sided with the Confederacy, even though the Southern pressures were intense. Grinde and Taylor discuss the reasons why some Indians sided with the Union instead of the Confederacy, which included earlier treaties binding the tribes to aid the United States and opposition to slavery in general. These tribal members who sided with the Union became incensed when some Indians in their tribe signed treaties with the Confederacy that allied the entire tribe to fight for the South. They felt that it was unfair for individual tribesmen to commit their entire Nation to the Confederacy, when, in actuality, tribe members had differing opinions about the war.

According to Hurt, the Lower Creeks who owned slaves and participated in the American economy were more ideologically in line with the Southern cause, while the Upper Creeks who lived isolated, traditional lives and received their stipends from the United States government favored the Union. Hurt also acknowledged that individuals existed in both kinds of towns who had ideas different from the majority though, and sometimes even members of the same family fought for different sides. Inside some towns, factions formed and began their own battles. At the beginning of the war, approximately half of the Creeks allied themselves with the Confederacy, because of similar values and because of the financial incentives that Pike promised them after the Confederate victory. As the Union began to win the war, the Creek Nation, in general, lessened its support for the South. In 1863, the Battle of Honey Springs effectively ended the major fighting in Indian Territory as the Union took control of most of the area. Nonetheless, as Hurt says, many pro-Southern Creeks refused to give up their fighting and fled to southern Indian Territory or across the Red River, where they continued a guerilla war against the North.

After the war, the United States treated all the Creeks the same, whether they had been pro-Union or pro-Confederacy. As punishment for Creek tribal members aiding the Confederacy, the United States signed the "Reconstruction Treaty" with the tribe in 1866. This treaty most notably outlawed slavery, gave the western half of their lands to the United States for Plains Indians and other Native Americans' use, and allowed railroads to be built through Creek land. According to historians Grinde and Taylor, the Creeks and Seminoles were the least discriminatory toward African-Americans of the Five Nations, both before and after the Civil War. The Creek and Seminole tribes allowed their former slaves to become full citizens of the tribe immediately after the war. This differed from other tribes, such as the Cherokee, who placed a few more restrictions on citizenship for their former slaves, and the Choctaw and Chickasaw, who were the most resistant to allowing their freedmen to become citizens.

The Creek and Seminole progressiveness toward African-Americans regarding citizenship was also evident in the Creeks' and Seminoles' interactions with and treatment of their freedmen. Grinde and Taylor note that the Creeks even encouraged former slaves to become politically involved in the Creek

I. Popular Histories of Oklahoma Origins

National Council. In 1875, four out of the forty-six Creek towns had former slaves as delegates. These freedmen felt like they were members of the tribe because they had grown up in their tribe's culture, speaking the native language and following the native traditions, like the Indian members of their tribe. This kindness and acceptance of former slaves lasted until railroads brought more commerce and settlers to Indian Territory in the 1870s and 1880s. At this time, the newly emerging commerce caused Creeks to disapprove of all settlers in the area, including both whites and African-Americans.

In addition to being forced to free their slaves, the Creeks lost half of their territory in the "Reconstruction Treaty." By the time the war was over, the fighting from those four years had destroyed a large portion of the Creek lands. Returning Creeks often found that their homes were unavailable, having been either destroyed in the war or ceded back to the United States in the "Reconstruction Treaty." Therefore, they had to settle in new locations. Hurt writes that as a result, the old lines of Upper and Lower Towns disappeared, but distinctions within the tribe still existed between "Union" and "Confederate" Creeks. This line ran just as deep as the old division between Upper and Lower Creeks.

The last major provision in the "Reconstruction Treaty" forced the Creeks to allow railroads to be built and to operate on Creek lands. Hurt says that prior to the Civil War, most of the whites within the Creek Nation were allowed to live in the area to provide a service of some sort, such as educational services, medical services, or missionary services. The movements of white troops during the Civil War and the construction of the railroads afterwards brought in even more white settlers. In 1872, the Missouri, Kansas, and Texas line was the first railroad built in Creek lands. The towns of Muskogee and Eufaula were founded along this railroad and soon developed into centers of white trade and commerce. By the mid-1870s, railroad construction in Oklahoma had brought in a flood of new white settlers.

Hurt examines another reason for white intrusion: the large number of newspaper articles praising Oklahoma's beauty and open lands reaching the mainstream American public. Although most of the new settlers claimed land and lived within the Creek Nation illegally, federal agents did not remove them. Grinde and Taylor note that by 1890, whites greatly outnumbered Creeks in their own territory, numbering 109,393 compared to the Creeks' 50,055. Although the Creeks continued to resist, they could not retain political autonomy against these large numbers of settlers.

After the "Reconstruction Treaty," the U.S. government also wanted the Creeks to develop a tribal constitution that decreased the autonomy of individual towns. Hurt discusses this constitution. The new Creek constitution, created in 1867, established a Creek capital at Okmulgee, divided Creek lands into six areas, and forced the tribe to adopt a style of government that was a reflection of the larger U.S. government. This new tribal government finally allowed U. S. officials to impart their own governmental structure onto the Creeks. The new Creek government left the United States with one centralized, small group of tribal leaders to influence, rather than the many separated towns that comprised the traditional Creek political structure.

I. Popular Histories of Oklahoma Origins

The integration of American governmental structure into Creek government was more difficult than the United States initially believed, as some Creeks violently resisted in small-scale uprisings. Hurt estimates that approximately half of all Creeks refused to participate, which made accurate census counts and taxation impossible. As the new government settled, Creeks began once more to identify themselves, this time as either "progressive" or "traditional" Creeks, based upon how readily they embraced the new way of American life. Thus, the large division in the Nation continued, even though the Creeks abandoned the old geographic terms of "Upper" and "Lower."

The United States used the western lands taken from the Creeks in the "Reconstruction Treaty" as tribal reservations until the Dawes Act of 1887 divided up this land, and most tribal lands in the United States, into 160-acre allotments. Grinde and Taylor discuss the loss of the western lands and note that in 1889, settlers began moving into the area and claimed these unassigned lands of Oklahoma Territory in the famous land runs.

John P. La Valle writes that, initially, the exceptions to the Dawes Act included all five of the "Civilized" Tribes' lands. However, the overwhelming majority of white settlers in Indian and Oklahoma Territories wanted a state of their own, and in only a few years, the United States government forced the allotment policy on the Five Nations as well. In his "Defining American Homelands: A Creek Nation Example, 1828-1907," Hurt writes that in 1898, the U.S. government passed the Curtis Act, which finally broke up all of the five "Civilized" Tribes' lands into separate allotments and paved the way for the land to become part of the eastern half of Oklahoma. The Curtis Act finally destroyed Creek Nation autonomy and attempted to fully absorb Creek members into United States citizenry in preparation for Oklahoma statehood in 1907.

This article is drawn from and refers to the following sources:

Grinde, Donald A., Jr. and Quintard Taylor. "Red vs Black: Conflict and Accommodation in the Post Civil War Indian Territory, 1865-1907." American Indian Quarterly 8.3 (Summer 1984): 211-229; Goins, Charles Robert and Danney Goble. Historical Atlas of Oklahoma. Norman: University of Oklahoma Press, 2006; Green, Michael D. The Politics of Indian Removal: Creek Government and Society in Crisis. Lincoln: University of Nebraska Press, 1985; Hurt, Douglas A. The Shaping of a Creek (Muscogee) Homeland in Indian Territory, 1828-1907. Diss. The University of Oklahoma, 2000. ProQuest Digital Dissertations. ProQuest. University of Oklahoma Library. 9 Oct. 2007,; Hurt, Douglas A. "Defining American Homelands: A Creek Nation Example, 1828-1907." Journal of Cultural Geography 21.1 (Fall/Winter 2003): 19-43; Kappler, Charles J., Compiler and Ed. "Treaty with the Creeks, 1825." Indian Affairs: Laws and Treaties: Vol. II, Treaties Washington: Government Printing Office, 1904; Kappler, Charles J., Compiler and Ed. "Treaty with the Creeks, 1826." Indian Affairs: Laws and Treaties: Vol. II, Treaties. Washington: Government Printing Office, 1904; Kappler, Charles J., compiler and ed. "Treaty with the Creeks, 1832." Indian Affairs: Laws and Treaties: Vol.

II, Treaties. Washington: Government Printing Office, 1904; Kappler, Charles J., compiler and ed. "Treaty with the Creeks, 1866." Indian Affairs: Laws and Treaties: Vol. II, Treaties. Washington: Government Printing Office, 1904; LaVelle, John P. "The General Allotment Act 'Eligibility' Hoax: Distortions of Law, Policy, and History in Derogation of Indian Tribes." Wicazo Sa Review 14.1 (Spring 1999): 251-302; O l i v e r , Louis (LittleCoon). "The Sharpbreasted Snake." Songs From This Earth on Turtle's Back. Joseph Bruchac, ed. New York: Greenfield Review Press, 1983; Young, Mary E. "Indian Removal and Land Allotment: The Civilized Tribes and Jacksonian Justice." The American Historical Review 64.1 (Oct 1958): 31-45.

2. The Creek Nation in Oklahoma

"Delagates to the last Annual Grand Council 38 tribes at Okmulgee, Indian Territory" - Creek Council House. Courtesy of the Oklahoma Historical Society. Dr. C.W. Kirk Collection, #8828.

3. Marry an Agrarian and Knit Your Stockings Red, or, How Oklahoma Socialists Rethought the Family Farm

By Christopher C. Turner, Lunden England, & Steven Eiler

Socialism! Red Scare! Radicals driven to desperation! Armed Rebellion! March on Washington! Threatened destruction of an entire town! Compared to the Oklahoma we know today, the politics of a hundred years ago as seen in its news headlines were anything but stable. As the state was trying to find its identity in the nation, so were its people trying to find their identity in the new state. In politics, they would explore every option– from the capitalist ideals of the Democratic Party to the radicalism of the American Socialist movement. Who were these radicals? Where did they come from? What were they fighting for? What hope did they find under a red flag? And what happened to them?

In the late 19th century the land that had given hope to waves of settlers proved to breed turmoil rather than the bountiful opportunities they had envisioned. In the years prior to Oklahoma's statehood, many of the people of the Oklahoma and Indian Territories would experience unforeseen hardships that revolved around the plight of local agrarians. Ultimately the struggles of these cultivators would usher socialism into the Sooner State.

Just as white settlers made their infamous march into the heart of Indian lands, the territory considered "undesirable" was declared the new tribal

I. Popular Histories of Oklahoma Origins

ground for Native Americans. However, with their insatiable appetite for land, whites eventually thrust themselves upon these lands as well. Energetic white men seeking their own patches of earth quickly saturated this Oklahoma Territory, which officially opened in 1889.

In the early years after the land runs, however, prosperity eluded the majority that sought it. In its place they found destitution and suffering. Those who fell victim to these hardships were the small-scale farmers, with their livelihoods marred by burdens of tenancy and steep credit rates, and by low crop prices. No one seemed immune—from the cotton producers of Indian Territory to the wheat and corn farmers to the northwest in Oklahoma Territory.

In 1902 the per-pound price of cotton rested at a meager 6.7 cents, and the number of tenant farmers was on the rise. In this Southern system of tenancy, farmers were subject to landlords, to whom a steep portion of the harvest had to be surrendered. What little remained of the crop, the farmers were forced to sell at market at artificially low prices. An unforgiving credit system further antagonized the life of the farmer. As the grower waited all season for the harvest of his crop, he found himself with no alternative but to purchase staples and supplies on credit. In order to take advantage of this credit, farmers were required to put up their crops as collateral. Farmers also had to bear the burden of the "implicit interest" that accompanied this credit—the fact that the credit price of goods would be inflated vastly beyond the price of those goods had they been purchased in cash. Under such conditions, indebtedness was virtually guaranteed.

These conditions were common throughout the South. Spurred by this pitiable situation, agrarians mounted efforts to better the life of the farmer. In 1902 the Farmers' Union was organized in Texas to combat their economic disadvantages. As the Union broke ground, its ideologies spread to the North, and by 1903 efforts were put forth to officially expand into the Indian and Oklahoma Territories. This gave rise to the Indiahoma Farmers' Union. The group made haste in organizing across the two territories, adopting a constitution and electing officers. The members of the Indiahoma Farmers' Union held power as a result of their affiliations with previous political groups. For example, the Union's new president, S.O. Daws, had been instrumental in the Populist movement, which met its end in 1896.

From the beginning, it was clear that the purpose of the farmers' organization was to correct the injustices of the current system. Union organizer Sam Hampton stated: "The mission of the farmers union is to completely overthrow the system of robbery, and to inaugurate the new and up-to-date methods." Union members simply had to decide the means of realizing their ideals. However, not all farmers who attached themselves to the Union held the same ideals, a result of their various social and economic standings. The Indiahoma Farmers' Union included producers from two different regions, and more importantly was divided into two contrasting groups: the tenants and smallholders, and the large landowners who depended upon the labor of others. Ultimately this division dampened the Union's ability to effectively make change in the agrarian world, as each group had its own interests and priorities.

I. Popular Histories of Oklahoma Origins

On a small scale the Indiahoma Farmers' Union did produce some improvements. Employing facets of collective marketing, the farmers agreed upon a minimum price they would accept for their crops, a ploy that increased the price of cotton to 10 cents per pound from 1903-1907, an increase of 3.3 cents over the prices of previous years.

Although a step in the right direction, collective marketing was far from the grand solution farmers so desperately needed. As quickly as it had developed, the Indiahoma Farmers' Union soon encountered obstacles that would spell doom for the organization.

Union leaders forged a plan to purchase their coal supplies for the 1905-1906 winter season directly from the coal miners in order to avoid the inflated prices at local stores. Farmers were required to pay for these supplies in advance, but as the winter approached, the miners suddenly refused to sell coal to the Union, saying they were not legitimate dealers. The Union took its legal action to the national level, which included a petition delivered to President Roosevelt. By the time the coal companies agreed to sell, however, it was already the following March; the need for the energy source was diminished.

Opposition greeted the Union again when its newspaper, the Indiahoma Union Signal, moved its headquarters to Shawnee. Daws, acting as the paper's editor, applied to local postal officials to continue the right to distribute the paper at second-class lower mailing rates. To the Union's dismay, the U.S. Post Office Department denied the application. The paper's subscribers were to be charged first class postage rates, a financial burden which the Union was not equipped to handle. Six months would pass before the paper's former second-rate status would be reinstated, without compensation to the Farmers' Union.

Conceivably the biggest blow to the Union's strategies was the Panic of 1907, a nationwide economic crisis. The Panic arose from a currency deficit in New York, which left smaller banks throughout the country short of funds. Clients found themselves unable to receive loans or withdraw money. This event, teamed with the Union's other recent economic debacles, pushed crop prices to lows which had not been seen in years.

Amidst their economic woes, the sects of the Indiahoma Farmer's Union began again to pit themselves against one another. The small landholders and tenant farmers, by far the majority, continually questioned the motives and intentions of the large landowners. The very seams that held the Union together were rapidly torn as the two groups attempted to move away from the other.

An outside party's involvements were soon becoming entangled with those of the Farmers' Union. It appeared that an alliance was being formed between parts of the Union and the Democratic Party, a phenomenon which had poisoned the earlier Populist Movement. From the beginning Union founders had argued against an alliance of this nature, but it now fell on deaf ears. Consequently, thousands of agrarians severed all connections with the Indiahoma Farmers' Union. In 1906, the Union's numbers plummeted, from roughly 74,000 members at the beginning of the year to 3,000 by the year's end.

However, just as the Farmers' Union had sprung from the ashes of the Populist Movement, so another political association would rise after the decline of

I. Popular Histories of Oklahoma Origins

the Indiahoma Farmer's Union: the Socialist Party of Oklahoma.

In order to take hold, the Socialist Party of Oklahoma learned quickly that it would have to tap into the people's deeply rooted ideas about their world. Three of the forces the party had to contend with most strongly were property, religion, and racism.

According to American historian Garin Burbank, "the disappointed and embittered tenant farmers voted socialist in great numbers because they expected to acquire land of their own, not because they wished to share in collectively owned land." The Party promised that they would help small farmers to acquire their own land so they would not have to pay rent indefinitely.

Whether this is a purely socialist position is debatable, and there were, as Burbank notes, some "doctrinaire enthusiasts [who] stirred up major controversies by questioning whether socialists should be trying to confirm private titles to small parcels of productive land." Still, the cultural reality was that people wanted land ownership, and the Party would not gain their support without promising it to them.

The 1914 Party platform suggested a system in which small tenant farmers could work on Party-owned land. Initially the system looked almost identical to the situation they were already in with capitalist large-land owners. The primary difference was that once the socialist farmer "paid rent equal to the land's value," he would be entitled to use the land – free of charge – for the remainder of the time he was productive on it.

Whatever their positions on land ownership, the socialists knew that if their party was to have any political power, it needed votes, and lots of them. The avenue by which many farmers converted could not have been any better equipped for the business. That avenue was the church.

Socialism, an economic system, may seem to the non-religious person an essentially non-religious endeavor. To the religious person, though, socialism must be understood (like all things) through the lens of religion; to Oklahoma farmers, the linking of socialist philosophy with passages from the Bible became a powerfully convincing argument.

They saw anew in the message of Jesus a message of class-conflict, and of a hope for those of lower position to raised to a better standing. They saw socialism as a divine movement, the vehicle by which the Kingdom of God would be ushered into the Earth.

Churches held party meetings, and the party regularly invited preachers to speak at their events. Socialist newspapers printed prayers, and sometimes painted evocative dual-purpose images with their words. In May 1918, the Ellis County Advocate suggested, "when Pilate handed down the decision the master class demanded, they led the Man of the People away to the Hill of Golgotha, and there suspended betwixt heaven and earth, one of the first great labor leaders of the world gave up his life for his class."

A few staunch party leaders complained this sort of blending of ideas was diluting the purity of their platform, but they could not deny that many of their constituents had joined largely for religious reasons.

I. Popular Histories of Oklahoma Origins

Not all party members were of this sentiment, and some Democratic publications latched onto this. They accused the Socialists of being atheists. While it may have bolstered Democrats against their political rivals, it only proved to fan the fires of religious fervor among the pious proletarians who felt the need to prove themselves otherwise.

Not all Christians in the area embraced socialism, and some were not embraced by it. Oklahoma congregations largely affiliated with Southern Protestant denominations, and anti-Catholic feelings were not only privately held, but also publicly displayed in many socialist newspapers of the time.

Prejudice was not limited to religion. The agrarians had also a complicated relationship with race. While affirming black farmers as fellow workers and sometimes as fellow party members, many white socialists still did not want to have anything to do with African Americans socially. Two men could earn their wages side by side in a field, but they would not sit together at a restaurant counter.

A writer from the southwest part of the state suggested that if the movement succeeded, "whites will not be able to exploit the Negro," but then continued to explain that the result will be that the farmer free from white exploitation "will have no desire to live among them and will naturally move to the place best suited for him."

"The place" he was referring to was the South, where most of the poor farmers in southern Oklahoma had come from, whatever their race. Only a few generations (and in some places, only a few miles) removed from the bitter cultural memory of the Civil War, a tension lingered between people of the region.

In northern Oklahoma, the story was substantially different, at least on paper. Socialist newspapers openly railed against slavery (which they saw as an ongoing practice in the sharecropping system), calling its abolition a great, but still incomplete victory.

When formulating the 1912 party platform, delegates locked bitterly in argument over whether segregation should be officially sanctioned to gain more votes. A black socialist from Cogar, Oklahoma accused an outspoken segregationist of threatening to "betray the principles of international socialism" and said that the "voters thus secured would bring with them their prejudice and disregard for human rights." Eventually the delegation settled on a noncommittal statement that the social inequality was not confined to racial tension, but was primarily a class tension.

As such, white socialists were still accused by the Democrats of being too sympathetic to their black comrades. Many farmers who otherwise saw promise in the socialists' message continued to vote as Democrats because their racist sentiments found a voice in the Democratic Party that the Socialist Party always officially avoided.

The Democrats would soon blanket the socialists with more dangerous accusations, but not without some outside help. Far from Oklahoma, across the Atlantic Ocean, events were in motion that would greatly affect the course of the Socialist Party.

In 1914, Archduke Franz Ferdinand was gunned down in Sarajevo leading the world into the "War to End All Wars." America tried to remain neutral as long as possible, but we were eventually drawn into the massive conflict.

The outbreak of the war created obstacles for the Socialist Party. Cotton prices plummeted from thirteen cents a pound to just fewer than 7 cents a pound following the closure of the European cotton market. The economic situation was more drastic than ever. Then came the draft.

Even before the United States was involved in the war, the Socialist Party was compelled to make its stance on conscription known. During the Party convention of 1914 they proclaimed, "that if forced to enter the military service to murder fellow workers, we shall choose to die fighting the enemies of humanity within our own ranks rather than to perish fighting our fellow workers. We further pledge ourselves to use our influence to the end that all toilers shall refuse to work for the master class during such war." The First World War was viewed by Socialists as a war between the money-greedy capitalists: "The wars of contending national groups of capitalists are not the concern of the workers," they said. This stand marked the beginning of the end for the Socialist Party of Oklahoma.

In 1917 the United States Congress passed the Selective Draft Act. It required all men of legal age to register within their counties of residence. Many farmers, both Democrats and Socialists, feared the draft. It threatened to take able bodied men away from their families, who needed them more than ever in this time of economic hardship. With their official opposition, the Socialist Party was determined to help anyone, socialist or otherwise, who opposed the draft by creating a legal bureau.

In August 1917 tensions were running high. In one horrific episode, Chas. E. Logan of Muskogee County killed his wife and child before burning his farm to the ground. He then killed himself. Other party members gathered supplies and opposed conscription by destroying anything that assisted the draft officers. These actions ultimately led to arguably the greatest socialist rebellion in U.S. history.

They called it the Green Corn Rebellion. According to historian Jim Bissett, the first incident of the rebellion involved black farmers with ties to the Working Class Union and the Independent Workers of the World. The farmers engaged in a brief gun battle with Seminole county Sheriff Frank Grall and his deputy. Other members gathered to make plans to thwart the ability of the draft officials from performing their responsibilities "by burning bridges, cutting telephone and telegraph wires, and destroying oil pipelines." The extent of the rebellion ran much deeper, however.

Following these attacks, some of the socialists organized a march to Washington, gathering members along the way and eating green corn to sustain themselves. They hoped their massive opposition to the war would convince President Wilson that he had no other option but to remain out of it. They were too few in number, and conditions were not right. The hysteria created by the war worked against the rebels.

Between 1914 and 1916 the Party had witnessed some of its most successful times. Eugene Debs was running for president. Of the 292,335 Oklahoma voters who showed at the polling stations for the 1916 presidential election, more than 46,000 were Socialist

I. Popular Histories of Oklahoma Origins

votes. It seemed the Oklahoma Socialist Party had become a legitimate presence in the Oklahoma political scene.

But the violence that erupted in response to the war frightened Democratic leaders. Before the rebellion could get under way, actions were taken to suppress the revolt, and within a week it had been quelled. Posses supported by the Democrats in power hunted down the war protesters. One of these vigilante groups was known as the "Knights of Liberty." To build public support for these groups, the Democrats launched a fierce propaganda attack on the people they called traitors.

In a wave of arrests, the officials made no distinction between socialist leaders who fought to make changes at the polls and the militant factions of the Working Class Union and the Independent Workers of the World.

This appeal to public sentiment is what Bissett refers to as "politics of crisis." Bissett writes: "Democratic authorities felt confident that the Socialist Party could be safely identified as a public enemy." Democrats reinforced the need for such drastic measures in the crisis of wartime. Between 1914 and America's involvement in the war in 1917, there was public hysteria. Many felt that drastic times called for drastic measures.

The effort to make the Socialist Party a "public enemy" succeeded. According to Bissett, the Democratic leaders took special notice of the absence of opposition by the public following the arrest of upstanding Socialist citizens, with many instances resulting in the outright denial of constitutional rights. Incidents of suspects' being lynched, others tarred and feathered, and some imprisoned for indefinite terms occurred in various places. They arrested anybody they felt was suspicious in any way. The lack of public opposition to their actions only fueled the escalation of actions taken by Democratic leaders.

Three pivotal events took place and provided the fuel for the Democratic leaders to determine to rid the Sooner state of the "Red Scare." First the Oklahoma State Council of Defense was formed to help curtail dissent and the war effort. Secondly, the U.S. Congress passed the Espionage Act, and lastly the Sedition Act in 1917 and 1918. The former made any subordination a crime and the latter flew in the face of the first amendment by criminalizing any abusive language towards the government, any show of support for nations in war with the U.S., or the interference with anything vital to the war effort.

Democratic leaders had the law and the public on their side, yet their tactics resembled those used by the Gestapo in WWII. Loyalty cards were issued to assure the allegiance of any citizen suspected of dissent. One incident occurred in Comanche County when a man refused to sign his loyalty card and was taken by force to explain himself, but to no avail. He was forced to kiss the flag and take an oath of allegiance. He was then forced to perform his civic duty by being put on the school board, assuring that he performed his American duties.

While the Council of Defense performed in the shadow of the law, the "The Knights of Liberty" roamed the countryside looking for Socialist traitors. In Johnston County the local paper, the Capital-Democrat, listed the names of registered Socialists. The Madill Record published an article condoning the actions of the Knights of Liberty saying that "more such organizations would not be one bit harmful to the cause of liberty." With their names provided to the public and vigilante groups hunting them down, Socialists were in a state of fear. In the elections of 1918 the war hysteria had been too great for the Socialists and of the almost 50,000 Socialists who came out to vote in 1916, just over 7,000 would do so two years later.

The official opposition to the war, and the Democratic Party's ability to wrangle public opinion against the Socialists, left the Party with little political power. One Socialist gave his opinion of the mistake made during the war, saying, "In our excitement of the early period of the war, we made a mistake and it is injuring our organization at a time when we have the best opportunity we have ever had to get our political and economic ideas before the people." It was true. The Socialists lost their footing—by 1920 hardly any remained in the party.

In 1921, a political coalition, the Farmer-Labor Reconstruction League, formed to address the rights of farmers. The following year five members won public office. They even won the office of Governor, but they ran on the Democratic ticket; not as Socialists. The promising and hopeful days of the past were gone, and the Socialists would never again have a platform.

The Socialist Party was able to build a following in Oklahoma because it adapted to the problems and ideals brought to the new state by its members. Small-scale farmers—immigrants from all parts of the nation—fought an uphill battle for socioeconomic change against Democratic, capitalist giants, but their energies were squandered when their radical response to the war was met with distrust. The agrarians had joined the Socialists looking for answers. While it lasted, the Party provided an outlet for their problems and a position in the political world. With no answers, no party, and the same problems, the disheartened agrarians on Oklahoma farms were left still struggling to find their place in the new state.

This article is drawn from and refers to the following sources:

Bissett, Jim. <u>Agrarian Socialism in America: Marx, Jefferson, and Jesus in the Oklahoma Countryside, 1904-1920.</u> Norman, Oklahoma: University of Oklahoma Press, 1999; Burbank, Garin. <u>When Farmers Voted Red: the Gospel of Socialism in the Oklahoma Countryside, 1910-1924.</u> Westport, Connecticut: Greenwood Group, 1977; Marx, Karl. <u>The Communist Manifesto: New Interpretations.</u> Ed. Mark Cowling. Trans. Terrell Carver. Edinburgh, Scotland: Edinburgh University Press, 1998. NetLibrary. <http://www.netlibrary.com>.

I. Popular Histories of Oklahoma Origins

Socialist Encampment September 2-5, 1910. Photo by Tom M. Greenwood, Antlers, OK. (Mr. Greenwood died Dec. 3, 1910.). Courtesy of the Oklahoma Historical Society, Government Collection, #20489.

4. The Territory of Terror: The Outlaws and Lawmen of Oklahoma
By Sarah Evans, Cristina Colbert, & Alisha Kirk

The "Wild West." The "Untamed Land." "Indian Territory." Whatever people called it, part of what is now the state of Oklahoma had a reputation. Many outlaws through its history used the Territory as a refuge where they could escape the law and rest. Others, such as Belle Starr and the Doolin-Dalton gang, made Oklahoma their home and "land of opportunity" in their own particular ways.

Indian Territory was a rough place at the time of the 1889 Land Run. Almost overnight, the territory was swarming with newly arrived settlers. What was to be done when trouble arose in this unruly land? Nonetheless, many outlaws saw this confusion as opportunity. They could commit crimes and easily get away. In many cases, as long as the outlaws did not interfere with Indian affairs and treaties, they were left alone because "the law" at that time was the thinly stretched Indian police force.

Historian Glenn Shirley describes it best: "The battle against lawlessness in this raw country was really not a battle at all, but a long-drawn-out war, with criminals violently dropping out of the picture, and new outlaws continually taking their places, until the balance of power swung finally in favor of the lawmen."

Shirley quotes author and lawyer Dennis T. Flynn, who lived in Guthrie as its first postmaster and as a delegate from the territory to Congress. "Law? For thirteen months there was no law but what we made

I. Popular Histories of Oklahoma Origins

ourselves." After the Land Run, thousands of people began to develop the Oklahoma Territory, but most overlooked the need for law or legal structure, including not only murder and stealing but also to the establishment of streets and borders. Everything was in chaos. Slowly, within the towns, laws began to be enforced and living conditions were greatly improved but once outside the borders, it was back to anarchy.

December 1889 brought some law to the territory. A memorial drafted in Guthrie by the territorial convention stated: "The laws at present in force in the territory relate only to crimes against the United States and the primitive forms of violence, such as murder and stock stealing...There is no provision of law as to child stealing, attempted rape, poisoning....swindling, making or using counterfeit labels..."

Over the next year, laws and lawmen gradually took hold in Oklahoma territory. The first legislative act on August 27, 1890, made Guthrie the capital. Legislation was drafted in Guthrie to send prisoners to Kansas and the "insane" to Illinois. Shirley adds, "The area along the boundary between the two territories, meanwhile, had become infested with every class of criminal from the most deadly and ruthless man killer to the petty, cowardly thief. It became known as 'Hell's Fringe'." What follows are profiles of some of the most famous outlaws in Outlaw Territory.

Belle Starr

"Hell's Fringe" is where Belle Starr lived, became a legend and died. Belle was born Myra Maybelle Shirley on either February 3 or 5, 1848, near Carthage, Missouri. She grew up just down the street from the

James boys, Frank and Jessie, and their cousins by marriage and later fellow gang members, the Youngers. Myra had many siblings, and her brothers relished teaching her how to ride and shoot.

1860 brought the Civil War, and her family quickly took up the cause of the South, as they were slave owners who depended on that labor to keep the family hotel running. Her brothers fought for the Confederacy and even Myra was rumored to have helped out the Rebel cause. Glenn Shirley's book on Belle Starr tells a story first circulated by the Richie family that a young girl arrived at the house one evening in February 1863. She claimed that she had gotten lost on her way back home and asked to stay in the house overnight; she introduced herself as Myra Shirley. The family knew the Shirleys and their history and did not care for them, but they decided to put up Myra anyway.

Union Major Eno was also a guest at the house. He and Mr. Richie, a Union sympathizer, talked of where his troops were quartered and many other "interesting things." Myra entertained the guests that evening after dinner with some piano playing and left the next morning after breakfast. She claimed that she needed to get home quickly so that her parents would not worry unnecessarily. She thanked the family for their hospitality, cut some switches for her horse and departed for Carthage. The cut switches were said to be a signal for the Confederate lookouts and would have alerted them to the presence of Union troops. A short while later, the house was attacked by Confederate troops and damaged to the point where Eno was forced to look elsewhere for a headquarters.

I. Popular Histories of Oklahoma Origins

Another story has Myra on an almost Paul Revere-style ride to warn her brother of his impending capture. She was said to have out-ridden Union troops and have caused Major Eno to declare her a "born guerilla." Her brother Bud was a noted bushwhacker for the Rebels. He was shot and killed in battle in 1864. It is reported by many that she threatened to avenge her brother's death, so she took to carrying pistols.

One tale has her accompanying her father to pick up the body of her brother in the family wagon. A squad of Union soldiers and many townsfolk looked on out of curiosity. Myra was said to have grabbed her father's revolver, pointed it at the troops and shouted, "You damned blue-bellies will pay for this!" Naturally, the crowd scattered and Myra was left feverishly attempting to shoot the Union troops. Fortunately, someone had removed the caps from the weapon, leaving it completely useless. Myra was reduced to tears at not being able to avenge Bud, while the Union troops had a good laugh at her expense.

That same year saw Carthage and the hotel sacked and burned by Union troops, so the Shirley family packed up and moved to Texas where the Shirleys were again not well received or liked by their neighbors. By this time Texas had earned quite a reputation for drawing many unsavory characters and those looking to "lay low." Rumor has it that the family harbored the James-Younger Gang as they rode through Texas after a string of robberies and murders. While at the Shirleys' house, Cole and Myra are said to have become romantically involved, but Myra married Jim Reed in 1866, a man with a reputation of his own. Despite many legal documents stating that fact, authors still claim that her first husband was actually Cole Younger, whom Myra grew up with in Carthage, and that they were married on horseback with the James gang looking on. Younger was even rumored to have fathered her first child, but he and Myra denied this up until her death.

Reed soon began living up to his reputation as a gambler and a thief. He often left Myra at home with the children while he engaged in criminal activity from Texas to Arkansas. In Indian Territory he joined up with the Starr Gang, well-known to have connections with the James-Younger Gang. The Starr Gang was also infamous in the Territory for horse and cattle thieving, a federal offense. The gang would take the pilfered livestock and sell them along the border to the "white fence," more commonly known as the Boomers, who would give them a good price.

Jim became a fugitive in 1869 after he shot some men who killed another member of his gang. The family packed up their children and moved to California, where Jim quickly fell back into his old habits and returned to gang life. After the local police caught up with him and charged him with money laundering and evading Arkansas murder charges, the family fled back to Texas, where they began living on the Shirley farm. Once there Jim abandoned the family and took a mistress in Indian Territory, where he stole at least $30,000 from Watt Grayson, a wealthy judge for the Creek Nation. Myra was rumored to have been involved in the robbery and to have been dressed as a man, but this was never proven. On August 9, 1874, Jim Reed was shot dead after being on the run for over three months. A

I. Popular Histories of Oklahoma Origins

tearful Myra was taken in to identify her dead husband. Jim's death left her in a deep depression for many years.

After being widowed, Myra Reed lived with her parents until 1876, when many of her family members died, leaving her the family farm in Texas. She quickly sold it, and leaving her daughter with her mother in Dallas, began taking trips to visit relatives. She somehow ended up living with Cole Younger's uncle in Galena, Kansas, where she began to fall back in with the "old gang." In 1880 she became reacquainted with Sam Starr, a good friend of Jim's and member of the Cherokee tribe. Within a few months, Sam and Myra were married. She moved with him to a Cherokee allotment near Eufaula, and Myra Maybelle Shirley-Reed became the five-years-younger Belle Starr. Belle named the area where their cabin was Younger's Bend, causing many to believe this to be a tribute to her first love. The couple lived peacefully for a while until their reputations began to catch up with them. They were the subject of much local gossip. Belle was known for her reputation as a loose woman and companion of outlaws while Sam inherited from his father a reputation as a livestock thief. Soon, any unsolved crimes in the area were pinned on the Starrs.

The couple was charged with horse stealing in 1883, and both were tried and sentenced in Fort Smith by Judge Parker, better known as "Hanging" Judge Parker. Belle and Sam got off relatively easy, with only nine months' jail time in Detroit weaving chair bottoms. They returned home after their release to find themselves more infamous than ever. Belle's mischievous side took over—she soon began to dress and act like the Belle Starr of legend. She began wearing velvet dresses and large gold earrings, topped off with a man's sombrero. She often rode through town on her horse Venus, with her Colt .45 named "Baby" out in plain sight.

During this time the Starrs were rumored to have harbored many fugitives at their house, but they are only known to have harbored a murderer once. A friend of the family was wanted in connection with a murder, so he naturally appealed to the Starrs for help. They harbored him for four months until officers tracked him down. The man drowned while trying to swim to freedom in the Poteau River. This only helped to fuel myths about the Starrs.

Sam was accused of a series of robberies in 1886 and spent much of his time that year on the run from the Indian police, hiding out in the woods and brush around his cabin. During this time, Belle was also accused of a robbery and was taken to Fort Smith to be tried. After posting bail, she posed for photographs with other famous outlaws, which cemented her reputation. She gave many newspaper interviews and even went as far as to whip a reporter in the courtroom who she felt had published lies about her. Even after her courtroom display, Belle was exonerated of the charges and released. She returned home to find that Indian police had shot and injured Sam and had murdered her horse. She then took Sam to Fort Smith where he paid his bond and was released. While there, she performed at the town fair by showing off her shooting skills and performing in a Wild West show.

That Christmas the Starr family attended a party near their home thrown by some friends. While there, Sam was confronted by Frank West, the Indian policeman who had hunted him earlier in the year.

I. Popular Histories of Oklahoma Origins

Sam and West began arguing and both shot each other fatally in front of Belle and her children. This tragedy cost Belle her second or perhaps third, husband and their land, since she was not a full citizen of the Cherokee tribe. She soon moved in Bill July, a friend of Sam's and a fellow tribe member, renaming him July Starr shortly after he moved in. The common-law marriage was accepted by the tribe, and Belle was able to keep Younger's Bend.

July Starr also had many run-ins with the law; he was arrested for horse stealing in 1887. Belle, fed up with his behavior, decided to not help him out, so his bail was never posted, leaving him to serve out his sentence. Belle's son Edward was charged with larceny a year later; he was released from prison after serving a reduced sentence. By 1889 July was back at home and charged, yet again, with larceny. Belle accompanied him halfway to Fort Smith on February 2; she was ambushed as she rode back to her cabin on February 3. She was shot in the back with buckshot and again in the neck with a pistol. She was left lying face down in the freezing mud to die. She was discovered soon after by a neighbor, but there was nothing anyone could do. Friends of the family sent a telegraph to July telling him of his wife's death. She was buried the next day in a simple, nonreligious ceremony with her pistol and some cornbread, a Cherokee funeral tradition. Once the mourners began to leave the graveside, U.S. marshals arrested her next-door neighbor in connection with her murder. (They were said to have been feuding.) He was later released due to a lack of evidence and having a good reputation in the community. The murder still remains unsolved, but many believe the murderer was her adult son Ed, who may have killed her after years of abuse.

July Starr was shot and killed a year later by Heck Thomas after resisting arrest in connection with a robbery charge. Belle's son Ed was convicted in 1891 of bootlegging in Indian Territory and served a few years in prison. He was released after his sister Pearl secured him a presidential pardon and went on to become a lawman himself. Pearl engaged in prostitution in order to pay legal fees incurred by her brother, and after his release, she began operating several bordellos in the Fort Smith area. Her children's exploits gave Belle yet another nickname, "the mother of a dynasty of outlaws." Belle is even reported to be related to the infamous "Pretty Boy" Floyd, who terrorized the South in the 1930s.

Tall-tales about Belle Starr were spread mostly after her death by enterprising authors and journalists. The National Police Gazette published many stories about her before and after she was murdered, all completely false and fully illustrated. A book entitled Belle Starr, the Bandit Queen, or the Female Jesse James was published by an anonymous writer just a few months after her death. It was a work of pure fiction and helped to fuel the legend that she was a crack shot and "braver than Joan of Arc" and "more amorous than Cleopatra." It even claimed to include excerpts from her diary and personal letters. Newspapers like The Elevator published an obituary after her death. The editor of the paper claimed that it was compiled from notes taken in an interview given while Starr was still alive. The obituary tells the love story of Belle and Cole and how her family conspired to keep them apart, giving readers a romantic twist to the story of the outlaw queen.

I. Popular Histories of Oklahoma Origins

The Dalton Gang

The call of the West pulled many settlers across the country. Legends of outlaws influenced many to believe romantic tales of the West. These outlaws, according to Glenn Shirley, "acquired more of the dare-devil spirit than they had been endowed with by nature; when the call came for them to join with other outlaws, they went wild." The Dalton gang most assuredly acquired this super-outlaw spirit, becoming the most dangerous band of thieves in the territory.

The three Dalton brothers, Bob, Grat, and Emmett had more spirit than what was good for them. They were among the fifteen children born to Lewis Dalton and Adeline Younger, the aunt of Younger boys of the James and Younger gang. In 1862 the Dalton gang settled in Cherokee County in Oklahoma territory.

As many tales of outlaws go, the boys started out on the right side of the law. Bob was appointed as posseman, while Grat was deputy marshal. However on their last run with the law, the boys decided that honest, hard work was just a little too much. They decided to take some cattle and sell it in Kansas. While trying to make their first escape, the youngest brother, Emmett was caught when his horse gave out. However, when no evidence arose that implicated him in the crime, he was set free to join his brothers in California at their brother Bob's house.

This gang of outlaws knew how to escape. On their next robbery, they set out for the trains. While Bob and Emmett escaped, Bill and Grat were caught. With their brothers in jail, Bob and Emmett fled to their mother's place in Oklahoma and later to Tulsa. Grat, while being escorted to a train by two deputy

4. The Territory of Terror

sheriffs, against all odds, escaped. In a chapter covering the Dalton gang, Shirley describes the event:

Suddenly Grat Dalton rose from his seat with a jerk that woke his bewildered neighbor. By a magic that has never been explained to this day, the bracelet around the prisoner's wrist fell upon the seat, while the man pitched headforemost and with lightning rapidity through the open window…..the excited passengers, now all shouting and crowding to the side of the train, could just see the form of the escaped prisoner swallowed up in the blue waters of a running stream…all they found in the river bank… was the leathern thong and fresh hoof prints of a couple of horses that had evidently been kept waiting for the pre-arranged escape of Grat Dalton.

Once the brothers were reunited, they added more members to the gang. Bill Doolin, "Black-Faced" Charley Bryant, Bill Powers, and Dick Broadwell all joined up. The new gang's first crime was May 9, 1891: they decided to hold up the Santa Fe passenger train in the Cherokee Outlet.

With law enforcement at low ebb, tracking outlaws became difficult in the open land of Oklahoma. There were few railways, towns, and ways to communicate. This set the Daltons up with an ideal territory for terror. The Dalton gang was able to ride through the territory escaping militias who came after them. On one occasion, the gang was able to successfully rob a train that had no ability to communicate with police and was forced to continue until the next stop.

In July 1891 Charley Bryant became ill and in need of medical attention. While in a hospital receiving care he was discovered by Ed Short, who

I. Popular Histories of Oklahoma Origins

had recognized his photo as one of the men who rode with the Dalton gang. He quickly seized Bryant, boarding him on a train set for Guthrie. Another difficulty in Oklahoma Territory was what to do with a captured outlaw. There was not always a jail for them, which forced officers to travel with the prisoner. This caused a number of difficulties, especially the problem of the outlaw's gang coming for a rescue.

An almost unbelievable escape was in, fact Charley Bryant's on the train to Guthrie. Short checked outside, while another officer was watching Bryant. Bryant was able to reach down and get his revolver with his cuffed hands. Upon returning, however, Short noticed Bryant with a gun, and shooting began. Both ended up dead. This sudden killing sent the gang into hiding.

Oklahoma was known as a wide-open country with lots of untamed land. The Daltons used this to their advantage. The Daltons, in fact, had two hideouts, so that if one was found, there was always another. Glenn Shirley describes the Daltons' hideouts in Oklahoma in his book Six-gun and Silver Star. The hideouts were small clumps of trees about eighteen feet square with a wide-open view of surroundings so gang members could see if anyone was coming. Quarters were made up of one dugout room with six bunks. There were also holes around the room making it easier for escape if someone had come across them. One dugout was southwest of Kingfisher, while the other lay just over the eastern border of Payne County.

The gang continued robbing wherever they could with little or no consequences. In October 1892, however, all that came to an end. Ever in competition

4. The Territory of Terror

with the James Younger gang, Bob Dalton decided to commit the grandest robbery ever. The Dalton gang was going to rob two banks at the same time, in the same town—Coffeyville, Kansas. Many stories arose of how the actual event took place. General facts, however, remain. The Dalton gang decided to rob the First National Bank and C.M. Condon & Co.'s in broad daylight. This was their downfall. While walking from their horses to the banks, although disguised, they were recognized. Suddenly alarm erupted in the town plaza while the men were robbing the bank. Just as two customers entered, unaware of the robbery, shots followed them into the bank. The battle had begun. Several men from town rallied to fight the gang. An all-out war had begun in the streets of Coffeyville. Bob and Grat Dalton along with Dick Broadwell and Bill Powers were all killed in the bloody street battle in the streets.

Emmett, though wounded, survived and was sent to prison where he confessed to the different crimes the gang had committed over the years. Lawmen and citizens both rejoiced at the end of this reign of terror. The rejoicing was not long-lived, though. Yet to come was another unruly gang of outlaws.

The Doolin Gang

One key person was absent from the fight that brought down the Dalton gang, and this was Bill Doolin. Having every intention of helping commit the robbery, Doolin never made it. On the way Doolin's horse became lame and could not continue. Another rumor is of a "misunderstanding" between Doolin and one of the Dalton gang. Either way, Doolin was supposed to meet up with the gang after the robberies occurred. The gang never made it.

Doolin was well known as a Dalton gang member and, in fear for his life, fled back to Oklahoma Territory towards an old Dalton hideout. As Glenn Shirley writes, Bill Doolin could have taken off to another country, but he had "tasted the fruits of victory in gun fights, he had known the glow and excitement that came in bank and train robberies and he thirsted for the life." After eight years of riding with the Dalton gang, Doolin decided he could not give up his outlaw lifestyle. He continued on his path of murder and robbery with the Doolin gang. With the Dalton gang, Shirley adds that "he made a record for the longest criminal career of any outlaw in Oklahoma and his gang figured in more sensational and bloody escapades than any other outlaw band before them."

The very first person to join up with Doolin in a new gang was, in fact, a Dalton. Bill Dalton was visiting his mother in Oklahoma when news of his brothers' deaths came, and it was too much for him to take. Next to join were George "Red Buck" Waightman, George "Bitter Creek" Newcomb, Tom Daugherty Ol' Yountis, "Little Bill" Raidler, and finally, "Little Dick" West. The first business was revenge for the killings in Coffeyville. A letter was posted to the Coffeyville Journal on October 14, 1892,

> To John Kloehr
> (credited with killing three of the Dalton Gang):
> Dear Sir:
> I take the time to tell you and the citizens of Coffeyville that all of the gang ain't dead yet by a damn sight and don't you forget it. I would have given all I ever made to have been there the 5th. There are five of the gang left, and we shall come and see you....We shall have revenge for your filling of Bob and Grat and the rest....You

people had no cause to take arms against the gang. The bankers will not help the widows of the men that got killed there and you thought you were playing hell fire when you killed three of us but your time will soon come when you will go into the grave and pass in your checks....So take warning....Yours truly, Dalton Gang

The attack on Coffeyville never occurred. It did, however, stir up the citizens and lawmen, who expected a huge raid. Instead, the gang robbed a train nineteen miles away.

The gang continued to rob banks and trains all over the area. After the robbing of a bank in Spearville, the outlaws split up the loot and took off in different directions. However, Ol' Yountis became aware he was being followed and made mistake after mistake leading to his eventual shooting at his sister Orlando's house. The rest of the Doolin gang would soon reach similar fates.

Cattle Annie & Little Britches

The Doolin-Dalton gang was well established before the addition of two of their youngest members in 1893. "Cattle" Annie McDougal and Jennie "Little Britches" Stevens were a sixteen- and fifteen-year old pair of girls who proved to be a welcome addition to the gang. Annie was the daughter of uneducated, yet respectable parents. Some say her father was a lawyer, but most accounts agree that he was a poor preacher. Annie was originally from Kansas, but over time, her family migrated to Oklahoma. Jennie had a similar upbringing. She was born in Missouri to poor, uneducated, yet respectable, farming parents. Like Annie's family, and many others, they moved into the eastern fringes of Oklahoma. The town of Ingalls is where the girls joined the Doolin-Dalton gang.

I. Popular Histories of Oklahoma Origins

Annie went to a local dance with her boyfriend at the time. He introduced her to George "Red Buck" Waightman. Annie was amazed by Red Buck due to his affiliation with the Doolin-Dalton gang. His stories of being hunted by marshals and wild shootouts were impressive in the eyes of a young farm girl. Annie was smitten with Red Buck, and Jennie felt the same idealism toward outlaws. The fast-paced excitement of the outlaw lifestyle attracted the girls. They decided leave their dull farm lives behind and become official members of the gang.

"Cattle Annie" received her name due to her keen ability to steal cows and horses. Because of her love of men's clothing, especially large pants, Jennie "Little Britches" was given her name. Both girls delivered messages, bootlegged whiskey, stole horses, and kept a look out for the marshals. They worked together or alone and sometimes with others; they often completed domestic chores during the day and crimes at night. Some believe that the girls carried on sexual relations with the men in the group in addition to their other "duties."

Because of their age and gender, the girls were not suspected of being affiliated with the gang. They were spotted on many occasions carrying loaded weapons, but were simply overlooked as teenage eccentrics. Floyd Miller gave an account of two marshals who passed Annie and Jennie on a trail in his book Bill Tilghman: Marshal of the Last Frontier:

Tilghman and Thomas were riding west out of Perry and had a brief encounter, which, at the time, seemed without significance…Tilghman chuckled and relaxed. 'It's Cattle Annie and Little Breeches.'… When they came opposite the marshals, the men raised their hats gallantly and said, 'Ladies.' The "ladies" did not respond but rode on by with stony faces. Little did the marshals know that the girls were scouting for the gang. The men were warned of the marshals' close proximity and escaped capture.

Nonetheless, it didn't take long for marshals to pick up on the relationship between the gang and "Cattle" Annie and Jennie "Little Britches." Soon after the marshals' encounter with the girls, the Doolin-Dalton gang committed yet another crime. Marshals were so close to the gang that they knew they had missed some clue. They soon realized that the girls were spotted in or around the locations of all the gang's recent ventures. This, along with the girls' suspicious purchases of ammunition and large amounts of food, led to the warrant for their arrests. Sometime between the winter of 1894 and spring of 1895, the girls were arrested. They put up quite a fight during the process.

Jennie and Annie were hidden in an abandoned farmhouse near Pawnee and saw the marshals coming. They attempted to escape. Annie jumped out a window, directly into the arms of a marshal. They scuffled briefly, but the young woman was subdued by the much stronger man. Jennie managed to get out of the house and ride away on her horse. She was pursued by another marshal. She fired several shots at him but never hit her target. Not wanting to be held accountable for shooting a teenage girl, the marshal shot and killed Jennie's horse. She still didn't give in. She hit, kicked, and scratched until the marshal finally got her under control. It has been alleged that the marshal put Jennie over his knee and spanked her before hauling them both to jail.

The girls were charged for their involvement with the Doolin-Dalton gang, as well as horse theft and other miscellaneous charges. During this trial, the girls kept up their "outlaw" attitude. They were defiant and rude to the judge and officers of the court. They were convicted on the horse stealing charges and sentenced to two years in a reformatory school in Farmington, Massachusetts. Once the girls left Oklahoma, they seemed to have dropped off the radar. Rumors still circulate as to how their lives played out and ended, but nothing has ever been confirmed. The girls remain a part of Oklahoma's outlaw history and their story was told in a song written at the time:

> There was a fair girl, her father was poor,
> An honest and God-fearing man;
> But his daughter was lonesome
> and followed the lure
> Of a boy in a bad outlaw band.
> Poor Cattle Annie, they took her away,
> They put her in prison, nobody knows where;
> Poor Cattle Annie, they cut off her hair,
> She was a good girl 'til they led her astray.
> Cattle Annie jumped out of the window, they say
> And shot at the men on her trail;
> Little Breeches was caught as she hurried away,
> Cattle Annie's brave fighting did fail.
> Poor Cattle Annie, they took her away,
> They put her in prison, nobody knows where;
> Poor Cattle Annie, they cut off her hair,
> She was a good girl 'til they led her astray.

The Three Guardsmen

The arrest and imprisonment of Cattle Annie and Little Britches was a huge blow to the Dalton-Doolin gang. The girls had been their eyes, ears, and gofers, without them the gang had trouble escaping some of the most well-known marshals who were hot on their trails. Between 1889 and 1898 these men captured so many criminals and reformed so many towns that they were referred to as the Three Guardsmen. They were Bill Tilghman, Henry Andrew "Heck" Thomas, and Chris Madsen. Together, with the help of other marshals and law enforcement, these men were responsible for the clean up of the Oklahoma Territory. The marshals of this time were almost the equivalent of modern-day bounty hunters. They tracked the most notorious outlaws who had the largest bounties on their heads.

Bill Tilghman was one of the marshals responsible for the capture of Jennie and Annie (Steve Burke was the other). He figured out that they were a link to the Dalton-Doolin gang. Tilghman was raised in the West and accustomed to guns and outlaws. He became a scout for the army in 1874. He eventually settled in Dodge City in 1875 at the age of twenty-one. While there he held such positions as deputy sheriff, undersheriff, and city marshal. In 1892 he was appointed as a U.S. Marshal.

The second marshal, Heck Thomas, was born in Georgia in 1850. At the young age of twelve, Heck became a courier in the army. As he aged, Heck's love of a good fight drove him to Texas where he became a Texas Ranger in 1875. He made such a name for himself that he was handpicked to become a deputy U.S. Marshal in 1886. He was soon transferred to the Indian Territory and joined forces with Bill Tilghman.

Chris Madsen, the final Guardsman, was born in Schleswig, Denmark, in 1851. He claimed to have been a soldier in the Danish Army before immigrating to the United States in 1876. He soon joined the U.S. Army and fought Indians in many

I. Popular Histories of Oklahoma Origins

famous battles. He was also a member of Teddy Roosevelt's Rough Riders during the Spanish-American War. By 1889 Madsen had already began his work with Thomas and Tilghman, but didn't officially become a U.S. Deputy Marshal until 1891.

During 1893, two of the "guardsmen" were noted with bringing order to a particularly bad part of Perry known as Hell's Half Acre. Developed quickly after the Land Run of 1892, Hell's Half Acre was filled with more than 25,000 people, but also with 110 saloons, gambling houses and dance halls. It was reportedly a place where at least two men were killed every three days. In October Thomas and Tilghman, along with other marshals, raided the town. It didn't take long for the marshals to clear the town of many of the people and illegal establishments. Even after they had been relieved of their duties in Perry, Thomas and Tilghman stayed behind to do some "fine tuning." Throughout the winter of 1893-94, they completely rid the town of unlawful activity.

During their reign, the Three Guardsmen were held responsible for more than 300 deaths or captures of outlaws. However notable this may seem, their claim to fame was the extinguishing of the Doolin-Dalton Gang. Between 1892 and 1898 they were at the head of the many posses of marshals that began picking the members off, one by one. Over the years they gradually killed members during many of their robberies.

Bill Tilghman killed "Little" Bill Raidler and personally captured Bill Doolin in January 1896. Doolin escaped, only to be killed by Heck Thomas in August. Doolin had told his wife to ride down the road with their daughter to a spring near Lawson, Oklahoma, and he would join them soon. Thomas and his men surrounded Doolin before he got the chance. Feeling cornered, Doolin raised his gun but was brought down by a barrage of bullets.

"Dynamite" Dick Clifton and "Little" Dick West were the last members to be killed. They were shot by Chris Madsen in 1897 and 1898, respectively. "Little Dick" lived, but after being released from a Missouri prison in 1921, he never returned to Oklahoma, where he had ridden, robbed and murdered with the infamous Doolin Gang. In 1924 he was shot and killed while resisting arrest after a bank robbery in Joplin, Missouri. He was the last member of the Doolin-Dalton gang.

Conclusion

From the time just before the Land Run of 1889 until law began to take hold, Oklahoma outlaws made a name for themselves that has lasted for over a century. Belle Starr, the Doolin-Dalton Gang and the Three Guardsmen who hunted them helped to paint the picture of the lawless land that was Oklahoma. The outlaws' infamous acts have been immortalized, however inaccurately, in publications and films that have helped keep their legends alive. Belle Starr's fame came mostly through tall-tales and flat out lies, while the Doolin-Dalton Gang actually murdered and robbed their way through Oklahoma with the marshals in almost constant pursuit. The stories published in dime novels and written by the Old West's tabloid journalists have become a part of the folklore and sordid side of Oklahoma's complex history.

I. Popular Histories of Oklahoma Origins

This article is drawn from and refers to the following sources:

Miller, Floyd. Bill Tilghman: Marshall of the Last Frontier. Doubleday & Company, Inc. New York, 1968; Rascoe, Burton. Belle Starr: The Bandit Queen. Lincoln, NE: University of Nebraska Press, 2004; Shirley, Glenn. Belle Starr and Her Times. Norman, OK: University of Oklahoma Press, 1982; Shirley, Glenn. Six-gun and Silver Star. Albuquerque: University of New Mexico Press, 1955.

More information can be found at the following websites:

Cattle Annie's Page. <http://www.angelfire.com/la2/daydreams2/CATTLEANNIE.html>; United States Marshall's Service Historical Perspective. "Three Guardsmen of Oklahoma." <http://www.usdoj.gov/marshals/history/dalton/three.htm>; Legends of America.com. "Belle Starr." <http://www.legendsofamerica.com/photos-outlaws/BelleStarr2-500.jpg>

4. The Territory of Terror

Cattle Annie and Little Britches
Western History Collections, University of Oklahoma Library

I. Popular Histories of Oklahoma Origins

Bank windows in Coffeyville after Dalton Raid. Shows nearly 300 bullet holes from weapons fired by citizens and bandits. Western History Collection, University of Oklahoma Library

4. The Territory of Terror

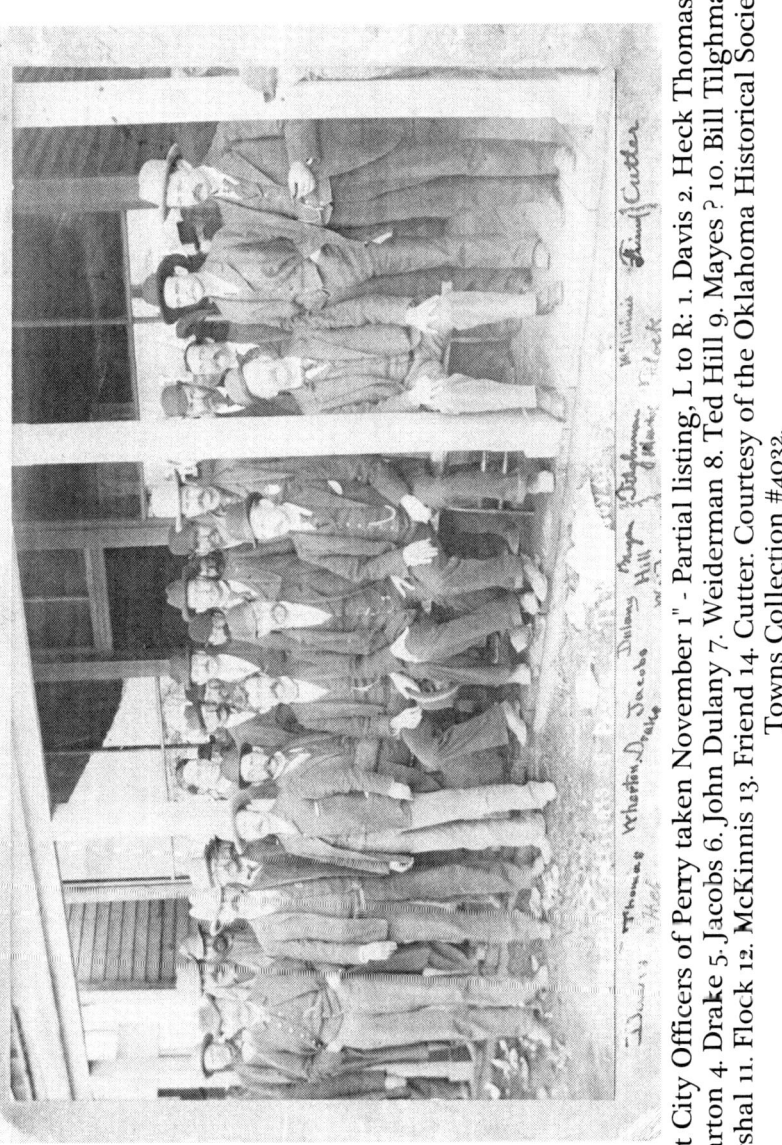

First City Officers of Perry taken November 1" - Partial listing, L to R: 1. Davis 2. Heck Thomas 3. Wharton 4. Drake 5. Jacobs 6. John Dulany 7. Weiderman 8. Ted Hill 9. Mayes ? 10. Bill Tilghman, Marshal 11. Flock 12. McKinnis 13. Friend 14. Cutter. Courtesy of the Oklahoma Historical Society. Towns Collection #4032.

I. Popular Histories of Oklahoma Origins

Belle Starr & Deputy U.S. Marshal Tyner Hughes. Photo by Roeder, Ft. Smith, AR. 23 May 1886. Courtesy of the Oklahoma Historical Society, Frederick Samuel Barde Collection #1356.

Part II
Reflecting on Identity in Oklahoma

5. I Don't Know if I Belong to the Land
by Steven Eiler

I was sick on the day they went to Rose Hill. I was typically a healthy kid and ordinarily would have welcomed a sick day like I would a snow day, but not when we had a field trip. My fourth grade class sat on a bus and rode halfway across the state to a one-room schoolhouse, while I sat on the couch at home and watched cartoons. Apparently everyone got all gussied up – the boys in their in their overalls and straw hats, the girls in their denim skirts. The children with more ambitious parents wore gingham dresses and faux-period bonnets. They packed their plastic baggie-lunches in a bucket rather than a paper sack. I sulked in my PJs and puked.

I had no idea what the Cherokee Strip was, or that the town of Perry existed, or why a field trip to experience hundred-year old pedagogy was educationally significant. I just thought it sounded like fun. But this time I had to stay home. My mom probably felt worse about it than I did, because she asked the teachers if I could go the following week with the class from across the hall. So I went and it was pretty fun from what I can remember – writing on tiny chalkboards, playing on the Flying Jenny – but I also remember feeling more than a little out of place. In the sepia-toned photograph taken to commemorate the event, I stand out as the awkwardly tall kid in the back wearing an oversized felt hat. I wasn't acutely aware of my stature or my costume at the time, but I only knew a couple of kids in that class, and I didn't really know how to talk to any of the others. Fortunately, we were under strict

II. Reflecting on Identity in Oklahoma

instruction not to talk anyway, so I followed the rules with no problem that day.

I'm told that we also orchestrated a mock land run in elementary school. If I was there, I have zero recollection of the event; I suspect more that I was sick again or out of town that day. There were no make-ups for that one. Over the years our mock land run came up a few times in conversations with friends – how great it was, or how dumb it was – but I always asked, "Are you sure we really did that?" Then, unexpectedly, I was afforded an opportunity to enjoy it all over again—or maybe for the first time, I'm not sure.

When my younger brother was old enough to relive the silliest method of mass-property acquisition this country has ever seen, I visited his school with our mother to watch him stake a claim. I carried the lawn chairs, and she grabbed the camera, and we made it just in time to see the kids scramble leftward (I would say westward, but they were actually traveling north). In the aftermath, wandering through the soccer field full of cardboard houses and covered red wagons, I was impressed by the kids' industriousness. Some had picked spots next to puddles (possibly for a water source, or maybe just to splash each other), and some had set up shop, trying to sell fake goods to their neighbors. The ghost of nostalgia moved in behind my eyes, and I ached inside to be a part of what they were doing, but I knew I could only observe. I was still awkwardly tall, but this time at least I had the excuse of being twice the age of any kids on the field.

Neither of these two events struck me as historically meaningful, just as exciting ways to spend a school day. Neither one seemed all that

5. I Don't Know If I Belong to the Land

peculiar either. I had never considered that a pioneer schoolhouse had any connection to the enormous multi-building campus I attended. I don't suppose I assumed all states had been settled by land runs, but I hardly thought about the state I lived in, much less any of the others. The East Coast was the territory of the cartoon pilgrims and the West Coast the territory of the cartoon prospectors. We were in the middle, and we were just ordinary people. We weren't on TV.

The day Timothy McVeigh bombed the Alfred P. Murrah Federal Building, I was running around on the selfsame playground my brother would later stampede. When we were called inside, I knew something unusual was happening because there was a television in the classroom. It was tuned to the news. At home, the news would be a good reason to leave the living room in search of more engaging entertainment. At school, though, it might as well have been the movies because it meant we wouldn't be doing any schoolwork as long as it was on. What I saw did not seem very real to me. I only knew Oklahoma City as a faraway place where we had taken another long field trip. I didn't know what a federal building was, and I had probably never even heard the word terrorism. My teacher said it was very serious and very sad.

When I casually asked my parents if they had heard about what we watched at school, they didn't reciprocate my lightheartedness. At that point in my life I'd not yet felt the weight of death. My great-uncle Harold had passed away, but I hardly knew him. Though more tragic in magnitude and circumstance than the departure of my uncle, the deaths of all the kids in their daycare and their parents in their offices did not affect me deeply because I didn't know any of those people at all. In an effort to try to respond emotionally to the catastrophe – or maybe just to complete a school assignment – I wrote a poem for the rescue workers on the scene. I called it "Dear Firefighters." "When the bomb was blown, our shame was shown. / On the day of the blast, our flags hung at half mast. / The people were killed and in their will / a patriotic sign from the past." The final line is telling of my poetic emphasis on sound rather than substance as a third grader, but also hints at a fundamental misunderstanding of what was going on around me. Six years later, in the wake of all the wreckage of September eleventh, I had the same problem. Everyone around me seemed to be frightened or angry or mournful. I was just confused. I felt terrible that so many lives had been cut short, but it all still seemed a world away. New York was a place they put in the movies, but I'm not sure I even knew anyone who had been there, much less who lived there at the time. My family and friends are all Midwestern folks, and I don't think I'd yet traveled outside the Central Time Zone.

    Both my older sister and my younger brother were born in Tulsa, but in the years between their arrivals, my parents decided to return to Highland, Illinois, where my dad had spent his childhood. I was delivered at Saint Joseph's Hospital in Breese – just outside of Highland – because the local facility didn't provide pregnancy and birthing services. There's a part of me that is happy to have been ushered into the world so near to where my father grew up, but I have a hard time feeling very rooted in Illinois. I have no memories of living in my birth state except for Halloween when I was two years old and my mom dressed me up like a pumpkin. By age three we

5. I Don't Know If I Belong to the Land

had moved to Wisconsin, and by the time I started kindergarten, we were in Oklahoma, and my brother was on the way. All throughout my mandatory education, I never gave any special thought to the place that I lived. It was a shape on a map, a place to come back to after visiting relatives, but it was never definitively "home."

Much of my mom's family is in Illinois as well, but they didn't start out there. Her father (one fourth Cherokee but without the records to prove it) spent almost all of his early life in Rush Springs, and he and my grandmother met at Oklahoma Baptist University. Once married, my grandparents had seven children. My grandfather was a Southern Baptist minister, and every few years the family had to pick up and move to a new town, a new state, even a new country (they lived a short stretch in Canada) to serve yet another congregation. As such, my mom and all of her siblings were born in different places. Every year of my life until this present Centennial year, the whole lot of us (fifty or more people in all) traveled back to southern Illinois to celebrate Christmas or Thanksgiving with each other because that's where my grandparents lived. After my grandfather died, though, my grandmother moved to Mississippi to live with my relatives there. When my Mississippi relatives moved to Tulsa, my grandmother came with them. When my dad's mother died, his sister moved out of Highland and came down to Tulsa as well. A generation or two later, just enough of the family is based in Oklahoma again that we decided to share Thanksgiving in Tulsa this year. It was strange. Being with my family was very natural, but being in my own house with so many of my aunts, uncles and cousins was a new experience. Even having the extended family come to Oklahoma didn't necessarily make it feel more settled in my mind as something called home. For me, it made it feel even more foreign, because to see my cousins meant doing something out of the ordinary.

I don't know if I belong here. I don't know what it is that makes a person definitively an Okie. Is it an attitude? An accent? Maybe you just have to be so accustomed to the place that it would never occur to you that you could possibly live anywhere else. Whatever it is, I'm pretty sure I don't have it. I love this state. Most of its history is horrendous, but not much more than any of the rest of the country, and the more I've read about it, the more intriguingly bizarre it reveals itself to be. The land run? The two territories? Who else has those? I feel proud of rose rocks "only forming in Cleveland County" even if I strongly suspect they're found elsewhere. I enjoy the fact that until 2004, we had a parasite with hardly visible petals as our state flower. My goodness, our state vegetable is a watermelon – flying in the face of scientific classification or even common semantics! To the person of such strange constitution as myself, it's a wonderful place to brag about to out-of-staters.

Maybe that's it. Maybe what it takes to belong here is to feel like you don't belong. It was, after all, the refuge of outlaws running from the government, of former slaves running from oppression, of American natives running from the encroaching immigrants. It's a place full of outsiders, and it's not quite old enough for anyone to be deeply rooted here. The land we belong to is grand – at least with a very forgiving and imaginative vision of grandeur. And maybe, just maybe, at the end of this hundredth

5. I Don't Know If I Belong to the Land

year of investigation and reflection, I can say that I, too, belong to the land.

6. The Story Beneath the Glare
By Elisabeth Brown

The pictures are crisp; if roughly handled, the paper may rip or even crumble. The black and white has faded to a yellow-orange. But still, the expressions of my ancestors are palpable. Looks of sadness, hardship, and pain fill the aged squares. I flip through the photo album, noticing that the hard expressions rarely change.

"They were ornery old people," my grandmother Nonnie mumbles under her breath. "Those Cookes would hit you on the nose for no reason." She's referring to her grandfather's side of the family.

The Cookes came from the Deep South. They owned slaves in Mississippi for years and later moved to Missouri with "hired help." They were stubborn and kept to themselves in the community. This is really all I know about them. Nonnie did not speak of them as openly as she spoke about other ancestors.

The page turns and there is the first smile I've seen in fifty pictures. "That's Momma Hamilton. She was my grandmother. The Hamiltons were from England and always refined people, soft-spoken. Sometimes my grandpa could be sneaky, but everyone loved him." Nonnie smiles as she speaks of this family that she loved so much. There are only a few more pictures of the smiling, happy lady and her sneaky, but oh-so-handsome husband.

As we continue through the scrapbook, the pictures begin to look more recent. I see the familiar face of my great-grandmother, "Momma," though as an older woman in her late fifties holding my one-day old mom in her arms. There are pictures of my uncle throwing a football with my great-grandfather

II. Reflecting on Identity in Oklahoma

and of my grandmother pregnant and standing on a desolate brown porch with her two sisters, also pregnant.

The last pages are turned. I am surprised to find my picture there! I am the only grandchild in the book. My deceased grandfather is holding me, ignoring the camera and smiling at my two-day-old face. I smile at this picture; I have one, my mom has one, and there is a copy on Nonnie's refrigerator.

Suddenly, loose pictures not glued in the book slip out, dropping to the floor.

"Whoops," I say as I reach down to pick them up. But Nonnie is quicker.

"Ah-ha! I wondered if I had lost these," she says, flipping them over to expose a tall, young woman standing in a flowerbed with a child clinging to her. Her eyes glare and her lips are pressed tightly together. Another picture shows the same woman, alone in a rocking chair on a front porch. Her expression is impassive, her eyes defiant.

"She looks mean, Nonnie," I say, glancing over my grandmothers' arms to stare into this strange woman's face.

"She was. She married a Cooke. Had to be mean to marry a Cooke."

"Huh," I say. I close the book, thinking the conversation is ended. A Cooke has been mentioned and generally Nonnie has nothing positive, if anything at all, to say about those Cookes.

"Her name was Anna and she was my great-great-grandmother. She was an Indian." Nonnie pauses, looks at me, and raises her eyebrows with a strange smile on her face. "But she would never admit it." This was when I learned that my Oklahoma blood runs deeper than I would have imagined.

6. The Story Beneath the Glare

Anna Gafford was a striking young woman. She wore her black hair in a bun most of the time, but once in a while, a lucky person found her with it running straight down her back, soft and silky. Her black eyes were said to be striking; she could haunt you forever with just one cold look. s

Anna was raised in the southeastern area of Oklahoma in the mid-1800s when Oklahoma was just a territory. At the time, the area was known as the Choctaw Nation.

Anna's mother was the illegitimate child of a white man and a Choctaw woman. She had come to Oklahoma from Mississippi sometime after 1830 when the Indians were removed from the area by the government. In Oklahoma, she met Anna's father, a Choctaw man, and they were married in a Christian ceremony.

Her father began farming in the southeastern part of Choctaw Nation, while her mother worked around the house and also mended clothes for a little extra money. A year after their marriage, Anna was born. It is not clear how, but Anna's father died shortly after her birth. Although Anna's mother was illegitimate, she was on the Choctaw role, as was Anna's father.

A single parent, her mother worked their farm, raising the chickens and the cows mostly on her own to later sell to neighbors and white men. People for miles around called Anna's mother a "half-breed;" after the death of her husband, many Choctaws and white men alike refused to speak to her. She was frowned upon and rarely could find help for the farm.

This caused numerous problems for Anna growing up as a child. Around age ten, she was reading silently from her primer in the local

II. Reflecting on Identity in Oklahoma

schoolhouse when three Choctaw brothers came in from lunch. In the story I was told by my grandmother, the oldest of the three boys spat on Anna's primer as he walked by.

Whether this was an act of bigotry against the white blood in Anna or just the deeds of a ratty boy, it changed Anna forever. She marched out of the schoolhouse that day, out onto the dusty roads of Indian Territory, hiked up her homemade skirt and walked the one mile home. She never went back to school.

"There was a fire in that girl's heart from the day she was born. My momma said it was the white man in her. I say it was the Choctaw." Nonnie pauses to take a breath. "Momma said Anna hated that Choctaw."

From the age of ten, Anna learned how to work the farm. She would go out with her mom early each morning and come in only for lunch and supper until the sun set. At that young age her hands became rough with calluses. Before the age of thirteen she learned to break a chicken's neck and prep it to be cooked..

With so much work in the sun, Anna's skin also turned a deep tan.. She wore long- sleeved shirts, even in the hot summer days, to shield the sun's rays from her Indian skin. Her refusal to look like an Indian became more intense as she grew older. Because Anna's mother was only half Choctaw, her skin was lighter and did not turn dark like Anna's did in the sun. Anna worked to keep her complexion like her mother's.

Not all people were hateful toward Anna and her mother. An older Choctaw woman who lived close to their farm would ask Anna and her mother to lunch once in awhile. Anna's mother would accept the offer, but Anna refused to interact with Choctaws. The hatred and rejection Anna had experienced all her life took a toll on her. She thought being called an "Indian" was an insult, and even worse was interacting with them...

"I don't know if my great-great-great-grandmother encouraged Anna to hate the Choctaws or not. From what I know, Anna's momma embraced Choctaw customs and culture. It was an independent Anna who refused to accept the culture that snubbed her." Nonnie shrugs. "I guess that's where our stubbornness comes from."

When Anna was sixteen, a white cattle trader visited her and her mother. The afternoon was beautiful with blue skies and a light south breeze. Anna was sitting on the front porch washing clothes in the big brown washtub when the tall blonde man approached from the dirt road. He introduced himself and explained that he had a herd of calves he was willing to trade for a bull.

Anna's mother came out and discussed the trade with the gentleman. By the end of their negotiations, the sun had fallen to the horizon. Anna's mother invited the man in for supper. Before dessert was served, the gentleman, James Cooke, had asked to court Anna. For once, Anna was not stubborn or uncouth. Maybe it was because she was ready for a change; or maybe she was drawn to James' good looks. Whatever it was, she indulged him and said yes.

James was a man of importance in his small southeastern Oklahoma development. He traded cattle and owned a farm, both jobs that produced him quite a bit of income. He was a man who kept to himself; rarely was seen in town unless it was for business. He did not speak much, unless spoken to, and he only responded out of courtesy. But James was also known for having a temper. He would whip boys who trespassed onto his property and beat the help if they messed up.

A few months later Anna and James were married. They moved to his farm on the border of Oklahoma (still Indian Territory) and Arkansas. From that point forward, Anna left her isolated life with her mother to become the wife of a white farmer in an all-white community. Not much is known about Anna and James' marriage. They had five children, two girls and three boys; none of the children were enrolled on the Choctaw registry.

One story that I heard as a child about Anna and James was that one day, Anna was standing in the cornfield when James came out to kiss her. But she adamantly refused to kiss him. Instead of accepting defeat and waiting until later in the day to get his kiss, James bent his head down and forced his mouth onto Anna's. But Anna shoved a wad of tobacco juice from her mouth into his and walked away.

This is one of the only stories about James and Anna's marriage. Anna was known to be harsh towards James and the children. She was also a stubborn woman who refused to attend church with her husband. Anna kept house and helped work in the fields, but she contributed little else to the community. While people in town were cordial to her, it was well known that Anna had Indian blood in her. With the prevailing prejudice toward "mixed bloods," she did not quite fit in.

After eight years of marriage, when James and Anna's youngest child was just a year old, James vanished. It is said that he ran away from Anna and her callousness. There is no record of his death or divorce or even another marriage. James just disappeared.

Rumors ran wild throughout the town. The one that has persisted is that Anna was just more pigheaded than James; when he realized Anna would never submit to him, nor let him win a fight, he left to find an easier battle.

Anna never remarried. She became sole owner of the farm and James' assets. She raised her children in that house and Anna refused to teach them Choctaw ways. They were educated in the local schoolhouse. The girls were married off at a young age, and all three boys moved east looking for work. Later, all their children would move back to Oklahoma.

Anna did not become more involved in the community after James and her children left. Some say she enjoyed the solitude of the farm. In fact, few saw the woman with the long black hair, sinister eyes, and dark skin. The livestock was sold off at some point and the cornfield grew over. One day, a daughter who lived a few miles away found Anna dead, at the age of fifty. She had died in her sleep.

"It would take me awhile to figure out how much Indian we have in us," Nonnie said when I asked. I wanted to know how much Indian blood I had in me. "But Anna never explained to her children her Choctaw roots. And not until my momma and I started researching our family tree did we discover them ourselves."

Just then my ten-year-old nephew Hunter ran through the room. He has deep brown eyes and black hair, with skin that is almost a russet color. He is large for his age, already almost as tall as my five-foot frame. .25

"Whatchya lookin' at?" he asks, grabbing the pictures from my grandma.

"Pictures of my great-great-grandmother," Nonnie explains. "She comes from the same tribe your daddy does."

"There's no color in this picture," Hunter says, throwing the picture aside. I smile at him, wondering if Anna's father looked anything like him as a little boy.

7. My Way to Rainy Mountain
By Sarah Buchanan

I was asked once by a Kiowa elder, "Have you been to Rainy Mountain Church?" When she asked me this question, the woman knew I studied the Kiowa language. I stumbled over it in my head, but my lips were silent. I hadn't been. I considered myself to be a good native person, one who loved the Kiowa language, people, and history, even though I am not a Kiowa Indian, yet I had not been to this sacred place.

"Not yet," I said. "But I have always wanted to go." I lied to the woman. I didn't tell her that I had never even thought of going to this place. I had never had the urge nor had the idea ever crossed my mind.

"You should go," she said. "It is a holy place. My ancestors are buried in the cemetery there."

"I will soon." Even I didn't believe the words.

I learned the stories of the Kiowa people long before and found that I was drawn to the history of their journey from the black hills of Western Montana to Indian Territory in Oklahoma, present day Fort Sill.

The stories of the Kiowa people are legendary. They are the warriors who cut the right side of their hair just above the ear to let their enemies know they were Kiowa. "Cáuigù" they called themselves. They are a people so immersed in community and language that story was used a means of prayer, fun and learning for all ages.

Rainy Mountain is where the Kiowa ended their long walk from their home in Montana. Located northwest of the main Wichita Mountains in Gotebo, Oklahoma, a small hill stands as a sacred landmark

II. Reflecting on Identity in Oklahoma

for the Kiowa people. Atop the hill is Rainy Mountain Church and cemetery.

I have read N. Scott Momaday's book "The Way to Rainy Mountain" many times. It sits on my shelf; slightly aged and tattered corners mark my favorite passages. I was even privileged to speak with the author about the book, yet it took the advice of a Kiowa elder for me to realize that I should see this important and significant place soon.

The legendary "knoll" is two and a half hours away from Norman, and not the easiest place to locate on a map. I asked a Kiowa friend who had been there before to drive me, ensuring I found my way to Rainy Mountain.

We stopped before getting there to take photographs of ourselves standing in front of the beautiful land. My friend pulled off the road and drove us to a rest stop. There stood a large plywood cut-out of an Indian Warrior. He wore a long leather outfit and held a brown bow and arrows on his shoulder. His long black hair was braided down the sides of his face. A hole was where the warriors face should have been.

"Come! Get out and take my picture," my friend hollered as he parked the car.

Laughing, I grabbed my camera and hopped out of the car. By the time I got to the cut-out, his head was already pushed through the hole. His smile seemed more jaw- clenched than usual from his excitement.

I wondered why this cut-out was on the highway, but he and no one else had any answers.

It's nearly two p.m. and I'm beginning to get tired from the drive.

"Can we get?" I asked.

"I was just fixin' to say that," he said.

We drove further up over a small hill and I saw a white sign. It read,, "Rainy Mountain Cemetery." I felt a chill up my back and down my arms. My face warmed and I knew it must have turned a slight red.

We drove past the cemetery and to a parking lot next to a small white wooden building where we stopped. The somber church was quaint and stretched around in a curve and the white steeple acted as a beacon for believers. Brittle land and an all-encompassing sky acted as the backdrop to the lives that have come through these parts. The car was put into park and the two of us were silent. My friend had been here before. "Many times," he told me.

"Ready?" he asked.

"Sure."

I opened the car door and stepped onto the gravel road; the simple covering dared not threaten the importance of this sacred land.

I didn't know where to start. The hill was everything Momaday wrote about: "Great green and yellow grasshoppers are everywhere in the tall grass, popping up like corn to sting the flesh, and tortoises crawl about on the red earth, going nowhere in plenty of time." He wasn't joking when he wrote that it was an isolated land with an imagination and will of its own.

There were plenty of cars in the lot, but no one was around except us. I walked toward the church and stopped for a moment at a large brown stone sign proclaiming the church to be "Rainy MTN Kiowa Indian Baptist Church." I walked up the ramp and to the front door. It was painted the same dull

II. Reflecting on Identity in Oklahoma

white as the rest of the building. I closed my eyes and grabbed the door, hoping it was unlocked.

"Get yourself inside, girl," my friend said to me.

Pulling the door toward me, I opened my eyes in relief and walked inside. The room was small, but peaceful. A service was being held. We sat close to the back and watched as the preacher gave a sermon. Suddenly, music began to play and the congregation, including my friend, stood.

"What's going on?" I asked.

"You're supposed to stand," he said.

Then they sang. It wasn't in English, it was in Kiowa, and I was excited that I knew some of the words. I hummed along as the hymn continued.

We listened to the sermon for a few minutes, and then my friend suggested we walk through the cemetery.

"This is where my ancestors lie," he said. "It's where I hope to be buried one day."

The grass was dry but the trees around the graves were lusciously green and surprisingly tall. He showed me the graves of some important Kiowa people. Chief Stumbling Bear's was the first. He told me that it was his favorite headstone to visit as a child because it made him laugh. The next was *Cotebo. He wasn't a chief, but he was the first Kiowa Indian to be baptized in the Rainy Mountain Church, and he said he remembered his family telling him that the town was named for *Cotebo.

We next came upon the grave of Chief Pacer. I found this one to be incredibly interesting because he was a Kiowa –Apache peace leader. And the largest grave was that of Chief Kicking Bird. My friend explained that he was one of the signers of the Medicine Lodge treaty, the treaty that forced the

Kiowa people to move to a reservation in Oklahoma. His was not a small grave by any means. It was a large stone tomb with a headstone carved out in front.

A gust of wind chilled me as I stared at the tomb. I couldn't imagine the harsh journey the Kiowa people had to endure due to that treaty that was signed in the name of peace.

Then I reminded myself of the Kiowa origin myth. It is said that they entered the world through a hollow log, one by one until a pregnant woman got stuck and no more could come out. That is how the Kiowa got their name Kwuda, meaning "coming out," later changing it to Cáuigù.

I remembered that Kiowa people have always been warriors, strong in spirit and stronger in community, and that there could be no where else in the world better to house their history and culture than this breathtakingly sacred hill.

And now if I am asked by another Kiowa elder if I have been to Rainy Mountain Church, I can smile and say, "Háu: and I never left." Because I know I will always carry that moment with me in spirit.

II. Reflecting on Identity in Oklahoma

Photos by Sarah Buchanan

7. My Way to Rainy Mountain

Part III
Shared and Sharing—
Experiencing Oklahoma & the Centennial

8. Oklahoma Centennial Bowie Knife
by Alisha Kirk

On November 16, 2007, Oklahoma celebrated one hundred years of statehood. All over the state celebrations—parades, performances, and exhibits—were taking place. Commemorative products were also made to celebrate the birthday. One could purchase almost anything including t-shirts, mugs and other items, to celebrate Oklahoma. But other unique commemorations were fashioned as well. For example, the Oklahoma Centennial Bowie Knife made in part by my uncle represents just one of many ways Oklahomans used their unique gifts to help celebrate Oklahoma statehood.

Ray Kirk of Tahlequah, Oklahoma collaborated on the Oklahoma Centennial Bowie Knife with Mike Miller, Jerry Lairson Sr., Brion Tombrelin, and Jerry McClure. All collaborators are members of the Knife Group Association of Oklahoma, organized in late 2003. The logo for the Knife Group Association bears the inscription, also on the centennial knife, "Knives, Man's First Use" in Cherokee. According to the group's website, their main purpose is to "educate and share our knowledge of knives through our meetings and sponsoring the one Custom Knife Show a year."

The Oklahoma Centennial Bowie Knife has an ivory handle carved by Miller and a Damascus steel blade with "1907-2007" engraved by McClure. The Damascus is the steelmaking technique that gives a pattern made by the layering of steel when it is melted together. Kirk was responsible for the guard between the handle and the blade, the butt cap and the spacer on the handle.

III. Experiencing Oklahoma & the Centennial

The Bowie knife was named after James Bowie, who in the early 19th century improved the knife after years and years of work. It soon became popular with hunters and trappers because of the particular shape of the approximately six-inch blade.

Ray Kirk, American Bladesmith Society Master Smith, has been forging knives since 1989. He is a member of the American Bladesmith Society, The Arkansas Knifemakers Association, The Alabama Forge Council, TOMB, A.F. & A. F., The Knife Group Association, the Sociedade Brasileira Dos Cuteleiros, and the Cherokee Nation of Oklahoma. Kirk was also recently presented with the Dee Daniel Boone award for the preservation of the art and history of the forged blade in Oklahoma. Other awards he has received have been for his knife cutting techniques, a first place hunting knife cutting competition in 2001, and a first place 8-inch tactical knife cutting competition in 2006. He has also taught a class on forging metal at the Indian Capital Technology Center.

A native Oklahoman, Kirk incorporates his Cherokee heritage into his knife-making. He has forged what is called the Medicine Blade. Each knife Kirk makes is signed with "Raker" with the "MS" under. The "Medicine Blade" is signed on the other side with Kirk's Cherokee Register number. The blades for the knives have been forged from a round bar of 52100 steel and then ritually smoked. He explains: "This is the blessing of something with a Cherokee ritual which involves the use of smoke and prayer. This ritual is to impart good spirits to the knife so that the blade may help the owner."

Ray Kirk currently resides in Tahlequah, Oklahoma, where he continues to work on his knives, always trying to promote the use of and education about knives. Recently, Kirk has been learning a new style of forging for the Brazilian Gaucho knife. For more information on his knives, see his website: Raker Knives and Steel, http://www.rakerknives.com.

Photo by Chuck Ward of Benton, Arkansas

Oklahoma Centennial Bowie

9. A Day of Mixed Feelings
By Elisabeth Brown and Sarah Buchanan

Native American Luther Standing Bear, chief of the Oglala Sioux, once said, "The American Indian is of the soil, whether it be the region of forests, plains, pueblos, or mesas. He fits into the landscape, for the hand that fashioned the continent also fashioned the man for his surroundings. He belongs just as the buffalo belonged." Oklahoma is the Native American's land of being.

Prior to the Trail of Tears, Native American tribes had lived among themselves on the land of what is now Oklahoma, sometimes in harmony and sometimes in conflict; they were the nomadic buffalo-hunters who resided in tee-pees. In 1838 and 1839 with the Cherokee removal to Oklahoma, more Native Americans found a home on the red dirt amidst misfortune. The Native Americans who now lived in Indian Territory had influences, some felt forced upon them, from European culture: English education, Christian religion, intermarriage, and manufactured goods.

In 1907, Oklahoma was established as a state, and in 1925, the roots of these native peoples in the land were acknowledged in the adoption of a new flag. The background of the state flag is a blue field, originally from a flag carried by Choctaw soldiers during the Civil War.

The center shield, made of buffalo hide and eagle feathers, is an Osage warrior's battle shield. The peace pipe and olive branch that lie across the shield are symbols of peace. This flag flies high in all cities and towns throughout the state's seventy-seven counties; it is such a powerful symbol that it hangs just a little lower than the United States flag. The Oklahoma flag emblematizes those who first settled the dirt, planted the crops, and learned the land for all of us today.

Traveling through the towns and counties of Oklahoma, one encounters names like "Tuskahoma," "Potawatomi," "Sallisaw," "Pawnee," and "Tahlequah." Such tribal names exemplify a history rich in Native American heritage. Besides the unique names that roll off the tongue, Oklahoma has much to be proud of in its Native Americans. The great Apache warrior Geronimo lived his last days in Indian Territory. Thirty-nine of the American Indian tribes currently living in Oklahoma are headquartered in the state. Jim Thorpe, one of the best athletes of all time, was a member of the Sac and Fox tribe. The name "Oklahoma" comes from Choctaw words: "okla" means people, and "humma" means red. The name says it all: Oklahoma is proud to be the land of the red people. Or so one would think ...

On November 16, 2007, Oklahomans everywhere celebrated 100 years of statehood. Throughout the year there were numerous centennial parades, concerts, and exhibits related to the upcoming birthday. These celebrations honored various facets of Oklahoma life, from the state's universities to its police and firefighters.

However, another kind of event, an event protesting the Centennial, happened at the state Capitol on the morning of November 16. But who would protest such an exciting event? The answer: Oklahoma's Native Americans. As Native American Brenda Golden stated, "Everything that I had seen in the press was cowboys, astronauts, land runs (and) oil wells. Where is the history of our people?"

9. A Day of Mixed Feelings

Native Americans across the state felt that they had not been given proper attention in the state's centennial promotions and celebrations. Oklahoma was their land first. They were brought here under harsh and dire circumstances; they learned to work the land and live off the soil. But Native Americans felt there were no ceremonies or special acknowledgement of the Native American ancestors who inspired Oklahoma.

However, Oklahoma Centennial Commission Deputy Director Jeanie McCain Edney stated, "Oklahoma history is certainly Native American history." She said the Centennial Commission tried to include everybody in the parades.

Statehood Day would officially begin on November 15 when all 39 tribes and nations in Oklahoma came together for a sunset ceremony. Yes, this acknowledges Native American's contributions for more than the past 100 years, but why have a special, lone ceremony?

The morning of November 16 was a bright, sunny day. The cool air did not dampen the spirits of the Oklahomans who appeared in Guthrie and Oklahoma City for the centennial festivities. In Guthrie, Oklahoma's first Capitol, reenactments of the day 100 years ago were being performed—from declaring Oklahoma territory a state to a parade in downtown Guthrie, citizens rolled out to celebrate the birthday of Oklahoma. But protestors also rolled out to Guthrie. Dressed in traditional tribal wear, they held signs proclaiming Oklahoma as Indian Territory. Nonetheless, their protest was smaller than one happening just thirty miles away.

The mood was slightly different at Oklahoma's second historic Capitol in Oklahoma City. Although it was a sunny day, a biting cold wind made it hard to stand still for long. The dry dust and grass blew into throats and eyes. At the Capitol building, we heard the words "No Justice, No Peace" chanted as protestors marched on the Capitol. We read a large banner reading "Why Celebrate 100 Years of Theft" that was carried at the Capitol that Friday. Approximately 500 Native American tribal members showed up to criticize the events that led to Oklahoma's statehood, including the experiences of Native Americans being removed from their lands and brought into the soon-to-be Oklahoma.

Dwain Camp, from the Ponca tribe, said "We're not going to do-si-do with the white man today. We're going to do this as long as they celebrate taking our land." Not only were they protesting the Oklahoman's celebration of creating a white man's land by taking it from the American Indians, they were protesting the lack of Native American recognition in the centennial events.

The march on the Capitol was not entirely about protesting the lack of recognition and celebration of injustice. Another banner proclaimed: "True Indian history in school." These Native Americans were protesting the lack of their history taught to children in schools today. The school children are not being informed about the unfairness American Indians experienced after Oklahoma became a state. Protesters saw the Native American symbolism that runs throughout present-day Oklahoma; it can be found in the flag, in the names of towns and counties, and even in songs and dances. But there is little mention of the land that the American Indians lost.

9. A Day of Mixed Feelings

Watching the event was an experience we will never forget.

We arrived at the capitol just in time to see the protesters walk their last leg to the building. As they walked and chanted "No Justice, No Peace," they carried their signs. Some of these read: "Land Run + Rednecks = Oklahoma," "Land Run was illegal immigration," "Latinos support you," "Resistance is not futile, we will not assimilate."

We tried to catch up to the protesters' pace, but despite our Indian heritage, felt as though we didn't belong. A drum was beat as we walked and chanted. We walked, but not as our ancestors walked before. We felt the peoples' anger at giving up their land.

When they reached the steps, the chanting stopped. A man holding a megaphone asked, "Did anyone get here with a drum?" The crowd laughed at the thought. The crowd was small at first, but by the time we got to the field with the small stage there were many more people in the crowd. The MC asked if there was anybody in the crowd who would sing a song. Suddenly, another man jumped up and began to sing in his tribal language.

When the song was finished, the man yelled, "T h e spirit of resistance, we need to help counsel the younger ones!" They began to sing, and we felt it in our blood, our bones—our spirit knows the language, but our mind doesn't understand.

"That was for burden," the singer explained. A man walked around with a bowl of incense, stopping to let people cleanse themselves.

Some in the crowd had long braided hair. Others wore their ranch attire. Many had feathers tied to articles of clothing. Many had red strips of cloth tied to their arms to represent their Native American blood. A speaker asked if we brought anything red to identify ourselves. The wind blew strong and seemed to say that it heard the Native voice, understood the struggle and would back their protest.

One of us tied red cloth to our right arm as a man continued to beat a drum. The man who handed it to us said, "It's the last one." A man whose hair was long and black, wore blue wranglers, cowboy boots, a black cowboy hat, and a buckskin shirt with no sleeves. On his shoulder he held a bow and a quiver of arrows, and in one hand he carried a tomahawk. Another man wore an OU cap and jacket. The jacket said "Sooners" on the back.

Feathers were hung in hair, braided or pulled back and tied into them. Some were on wooden poles and sticks that were painted tribal colors on baseball caps and signs. Protestors came to stay; there were lawn chairs, snacks and blankets to help pass time. We heard a man talking about the mock wedding of Oklahoma and Indian Territories later in the day. He said that he was upset that they were having a white man act as Mr. Oklahoma Territory and a Native American woman act as Ms. Indian Territory. The symbolism of the act bothered him. "Haven't our people been submissive long enough?" he asked. His friend told him that there would be two mock weddings, the one he had mentioned and another where the man was Mr. Indian Territory, but he would be gagged, an incredibly powerful message.

Marvin Watkins, 84 years old, was one of the speakers. She was introduced as an elder to talk about life in Indian Territory. She spoke about being worried as a young person about being caught speaking her native language. She said if they were

9. A Day of Mixed Feelings

caught they would get their mouths washed out with "brown laundry soap."

Another speaker was Cornell Tenderfoot. He proclaimed sovereignty for Oklahoma as a Native American nation. He said, "Takes all day and a year to talk about Indians."

We spoke with a Dakota woman and Cheyenne man about the event. We asked them what they felt or thought of the protest. The woman said she agreed with it. "It's truthful. This is us being honest about what really happened." Instead of answering our question, the man asked me what we were writing, after he noticed that one of us was taking notes. We told him it was for our history and for an essay. "My grandmother was Indian," I said. "So am I."

The man looked me up and down and said, "I read something that may upset you."

We had just met the man and he was already threatening to upset us. "What was it?"

"About your grandmother and how Indians are only Indian for convenience. I am Indian every day while others are only for the card and benefits. They only say they're Indian when trying to get a job or going to the clinic. It makes me ___," he said. The last word was in Cheyenne so we couldn't make it out, but we understood. "Do you know what that means?" he asked about the word.

"Yes, sick to my stomach."

His face grew angry as he spoke. "Nauseated," he said before turning away to speak with some friends in Cheyenne.

Sarah was appalled that she needed to prove herself. "I am Indian every day, not for the benefits, but in my spirit and life. Not for the luxury, but for

117

the reality. But I didn't want to try to change this man's mind about me," she said.

We walked away to another side of the protest where there were more speakers. One was the actress, Casey Camp-Horinek. She talked of many things. She told the origin of the term "redskin." She said that it came from white people skinning the Native Americans and selling it while it was still bloody.

She also discussed white people's ignorance of Indian culture. She demanded that schools tell the true history of the Indian people as well as not use Native Americans as mascots. At this point somebody in the crowd yelled out, "White washed history" and the speaker acknowledged and agreed with it. Finally, she talked of television shows that have white people in red face. She said she was unhappy with that fact.

After Casey spoke a man to the left of the stage began to yell. He invited the crowd to join in as they danced, and many did so. A few of the women dancers wore full length skirts made of a thin multi-color material. The women had bundles of cans and turtle shells tied to their ankles as noise makers and shook them as they danced.

A small drum was placed in the middle of a space, and everyone circled it. They followed different leaders for each dance, but all the leaders were men.

In the first dance the leader snaked them around the drum, and at times changed the direction of the train. As the group circled they would chant, as if singing responses to those who were leading. Throughout the dance, more and more people joined. At the end of the dancing, a woman in one of the colorful skirts walked toward the perimeter of the ring with tears running down her face.

9. A Day of Mixed Feelings

Christopher Topher, a senior at the University of Oklahoma and another attendee of the protest said: "Honestly, I had a true sympathy for the situations of the Native Americans before I attended the protest. I have always admired the close relationship that many Indians had with nature, and how that was incorporated into their system of beliefs. I considered the treatment of the Indians as the worst genocide that I was aware of. So, I was leaning more toward the point-of-view of the protesters, and I expected the protest to be a celebration of culture, as well."

When the dancers finished there were other speakers. One called the statehood celebration, "Centennial B.S." She spoke of proverbs in the Bible. "The last will come first," suggesting that God will return the lands to the Native Americans.

As the day wore on, the cold dry wind made it difficult to hear. Also, as the protest went on, the speeches became more aggressive towards whites, which discouraged us. The hatred and anger in the voices of the people made us feel as though there was nothing that could be done to help reduce the division between the two cultures.

The protest at Oklahoma's Capitol should be noted and serve as an eye-opener to the state's politicians and citizens alike. Have Oklahoma's politicians tried to reconcile with the descendants of the American Indians who had their land stolen from them? Native Americans mean so much to the state of Oklahoma; they are our past and our future. It is important to formally acknowledge the contributions and history of American Indians to Oklahoma.

Ironically, the bronze statue atop the dome of Oklahoma's Capitol building, is of a Native American. Called "The Guardian." It was sculpted by a Native American artist, Kelley Haney, and placed there in honor of the Native American heritage of Oklahoma. As The Guardian looked down on the protestors at the State Capitol that special November 16, it was obvious that such symbols cannot solve the anger and frustration of Native Americans all over Oklahoma. Other solutions might include a monetary reimbursement. Whatever it may be, American Indians are Oklahoma. We still need to acknowledge that in a special, significant way.

This article is drawn from and refers to the following sources:

ShopOklahoma.com. <www.shopoklahoma.com/native.htm; "Native American Group to Protest on Oklahoma Statehood Day." KOCO News. <http://www.koco.com/news/14524129/detail.html>; "No Justice, No Peace." RezNet. <http://www.reznetnews.org/article/ap/&%23039;no-justice,-no-peace&%23039>

9. A Day of Mixed Feelings

During the protest. Photo by Sarah Buchanan.

10. Sweet Treats & Good Eats: A Look at Oklahoma's Unique Restaurants

By Alisha Kirk,
Elizabeth Brown,
Sarah Buchanan &,
Christopher Turner

"Homecookin'" is always the best cooking, and "Ma and Pop" cafes can be found in nearly every town in Oklahoma. They are not the fancy establishments of New York or Paris, or the uniformed plates with interchangeable side dishes in the corporate restaurants near every major exit on any U.S. highway. Instead, many of these cafes started with nothing more than someone's grandmother and a grill in the back of the family gas station or local bar. The home cooked meals provided the working man and woman with an escape from the monotony of the "box lunch," the retired farmer with endless nickel-a-cup coffee, and the communities with a social hub. The best of these family dives have persisted, and we have chosen three unique restaurants to showcase the delicious simplicity of Oklahoma's working-man cuisine.

Van's Pig Stand

One meal in America, always guarantees to get people socializing, and Bar-B-Q is what we do right. In Norman if you want real Bar-B-Q and good Bar-B-Q, you to Van's Pig Stand on Classen.

Van's Bar-B-Q originated in Wewoka in 1928 serving pig sandwiches and ribs. In 1929 the eatery in Seminole was opened. The Shawnee store was added in 1930, and in November 1994, Van brought his wonderful Bar-B-Q to Norman. Van's quickly became a favorite in the Sooner nation, voted "Norman's Best Bar-B-Q" in the local Gazette. Van's offers catering as well as accommodations for private parties. Today, Van's is still owned and operated by the very same family who opened it.

Van's offers a wide variety of food selections. A customer may choose to order on their own or group together with other people in the party to split some wonderful Bar-B-Q. Different sizes of ribs, pork, chicken, turkey, hot links, and polish sausage, and anything you could want is offered as Bar-B-Q. The sides include anything from baked beans and fried okra to "curly q" fries. For a large party, you can order by the pound of ribs, brisket, and beef. And don't forget desert—homemade desert. Carrot cake, apple pie and pecan pie are all available in slices or a whole pie for around seven dollars. Of course, what is a trip to a wonderful Bar-B-Q restaurant without the sauce? You may purchase a pint, a gallon, or even a case of Bar-B-Q for your future barbeque needs.

Van's in Norman occupies an historic garage/filling station decorated with old car tags and other auto memorabilia. When you walk into Van's, you immediately are greeted with "What would you like to drink?" The ordering process has begun. With a large menu covering the wall, you are able to see all of your choices. You give the order and wait for your name to be called. Although the Van's has a walk-up counter for ordering there are also waiters and waitresses walking around making sure you are having the best possible meal.

The social aspect cannot be ignored when talking about a Bar-B-Q. With Van's food selections making it easier to share, the restaurant becomes a great place to kick back and relax while you eat and catch up with friends. The friendly service is obvious; while chatting, the waiters and waitresses come by asking to refill your drink, never hurrying you along, allowing you time to relax. You may stay for hours eating, drinking, and catching up with friends while never feeling like you are being rushed out.

What food is great in America? Bar-B-Q! Where in Oklahoma do you get great Bar-B-Q? Van's Pig stand. If you are ever in town, stop by and get a great meal with friends at Van's Pig stand.

Pops

Arcadia, Oklahoma, is a hop, skip, and a jump from the bustling, ever-growing town of Edmond, located north of Oklahoma City in the heart of the state. When the infamous Route 66 meets Arcadia, there one can find a special little gas station called Pops.

A white frame house replete with glass windows looks contemporary and out of place in the farmland of Arcadia. Surrounded by nothing but fields and hay, the gas station has a large parking lot north of the building. An extremely large bottle with a white circular frame stands in front of the station. At night, this bottle lights up in different colors. Pops' website describes it as a "dazzling light show of Times Square-quality luminosity…like a rocketship from another realm."

The exterior is all glass and white frames; extremely modern. Inside, there is so much more. Walking in, a normal gas station is nowhere to be found. Soda bottles of all sizes, colors, and tastes line the walls. To the left, an old-fashioned soda counter with bar stools and a grill. To the right, a counter where you can pay for gas and buy the normal chips, candy, and drinks. But who wants to pay and leave when this gas station serves more than snacks? A hostess stand is to the left of the door. The hostess greets you with a menu and, if you are lucky, you are led to a table. But, from my numerous visits to Pops, I have learned that waiting anywhere from fifteen minutes to an hour and a half is normal. Pops' popularity comes from the tastiness of food, the environment and friendly service. And of course... the enormous variety of different types of soda to choose from!

Over 500 sodas line the walls and fill the bins of Pops. The different colors and varieties create a rainbow-like feel to the luminous walls. A person can quench their thirst with any of these beautiful bottles. Their pop-off tops make you feel old-fashioned in such a modern place. If you forget to bring your bottle opener with you, not to worry—a waiter or waitress will be happy to help!

How can there be more than 500 soda flavors in one building? Impossible, right? Well, here's a sample of the different Pops' flavors: Captain Eli's Blueberry Pop, Cool Mountain Blue Razz, Frostie Blue Cream Soda, Jack Black Blue Cream, Jackson Hole Huckleberry Soda, Moxie Blue Cream Soda, Flathead Monster Huckleberry Soda, Ramune Sangaria Original, Sioux City Blue, Filbert's Blue Raspberry, Gordon's Blue Cream, Jones Bubble Gum... and that's just the Blue Heaven sodas! There's also Big Red, Cool Mountain Black Cherry, Jones Grape, Nu Grape, Fanta Strawberry, Gray's Raspberry Cream Soda, Green River, and IBC Cherry Limeade, just to name a few.

But in addition to soda, shakes and floats are popular, too! You just cannot have an old-fashioned soda shop without the floats and milkshakes! At each table there is also a wine list for the adults. Most people over the age of 21 stick to the flavored sodas and shakes, though. These seem to go better with the fabulous half-pound burgers.

Large burgers and delicious French fries entice people to visit Pops weekly. Soups, salads, and chili are also on the menu; Pops' chili tastes just like mom's and is worth the wait for a table! Not a burger person? Pops serves breakfast! Eggs, biscuits, and waffles are also popular items on their menu.

If you come to Pops and decide to stay to eat, which I encourage you do, shopping is an option while you wait for a table or your food. Hats, t-shirts, keychains, bottle openers, and koozies are just a few of the many items available from Pops. The shirts are fun, one with a Coke bottle on the back and the front reading "I Heart Pops." Pre-wrapped gifts are popular from Pops; a flavored soda is wrapped in a Pops' logo plastic bag with a keychain, bottle opener and drink coasters.

So next time you decide to take a drive down Route 66, stop in at Pops just before you reach Arcadia. With a larger-than-life, modern soda bottle out front, you cannot miss it! And besides, by that time you will probably need gas anyway.

Eischen's: Simple Man's Chicken and Okra

On the corner of Oklahoma and Second Street, at the Kingfisher county line in Okarche is a quaint little bar that has existed since 1896. Part grocery store, part bar, and part historical marker, Eischen's has nothing but a simple sign above a green metal door to suggest it's more than what it seems.

As you open the humble door, you are welcomed by the darkness of painted green walls. You look to the black and white checkered floor to be certain not to loose your footing on the sawdust while making your way to a seat. The jukebox serenades the place with a random selection of songs from Tom T, Hill's "I Like Beer" to Black Eyed Peas' "Lets Get It Started," adding to the ambiance of this kitschy country place.

You stare along the walls, taking in the enormity of clichéd items that blanket your sight. There is a beer koozie hanging from a paper clip above your head. You might wonder why this item is of importance. Pictures of horses and locals are to your right and a neon sign lights up the frames. Animals are mounted around the room—they won't stare, but the men in ball caps and Harley Davidson attire will suspiciously examine anyone who looks like they may be from out of town.

A waitress comes to your table and says, "Chicken and okra?" as if to say, that's what you're getting. She asks, "What you drinkin?" Keep it simple; they don't have any fancy imported beer or wine here. "I'll do a Bud," you answer. She shoots it to you straight.

A couple sits down behind you. The waitress comes to their table placing a pitcher of water and stacked Styrofoam cups in front of them. Serve yourself isn't just an attitude, it's the way things are. They offend her with a question; they're looking for some French fries. "Naw!" she says, already turned on her way back to the bar and before the customer could finish the question. The waitress returns with your beer. She whips out a church key and pops the tops right at the table. She makes herself scarce and in her place, a strange man comes with the order. "Here's your food and plates," he says, placing down a basket of an entire chicken that has been disassembled and fried, one of okra and fifteen sheets of butcher paper, give or take. The butcher paper provides one degree of separation from eating off the surface of the table. In addition, an ensemble of dill and sweet pickles, raw onions and bread accompany the main course. He trails away, leaving you to read, "I get loaded everyday" on the back of his shirt.

Looking to the crisp chicken, you're ready to partake of the red-dirt feast. Staring back is a basket of juicy, breaded bite-size okra and a stack of drums, wings, breasts, and thighs. So succulent, but it's too hot! You force it, though. The sweet smell of fried flour overwhelms the pain from the blistering grease pockets.

You see the waitress and realize your beer is almost gone. But she ignores your table, walking to a group of elderly patrons. "Hey, what are you kids drinking?" she asks. Meanwhile, you concentrate on a sign hanging on the wall above, proclaiming Eischen's to be the oldest bar in Oklahoma. Atop the napkin holder, a sign provides the history. It reads, "Peter Eischen established the joint in 1896, and it remained until prohibition. Following its repeal, Peter's son and grandson reopened the little bar in Okarche, and with time the name became synonymous with great fried chicken."

Finally, as the bar begins to clear out, the waitress finds time to shoot the shit with the customers. She sees you studying the walls, specifically the large ornately carved part of one wall. She says, "That's what's left over from the fire." She doesn't elaborate on the story, but leaves you to go look at the newspaper clippings hung on the wall.

III. Shared & Sharing: Experiencing Oklahoma & the Centennial

You look at the five frames displaying photos of the devastating fire. One is from USA Today while the rest are local papers. They each say the fire was in January of 1993.

As the waitress quickly cleans the surrounding tables, she provides a little history lesson. "The fire burnt everything to the ground except that section of the original bar," she says. It was hand carved in Spain in the early 1800's and made its way to the west coast during the gold rush before finding its home at Eischen's Bar.

There aren't to-go boxes at this restaurant and bar. Instead, there is an industrial size box of tin foil that sits at the end of the bar. The waitress would probably bring some to you, but you just get it yourself.

A man, sitting at the next table, asks, "Can I get the check?" She pauses, places her hands on her hips and says, "Yeah. Two chickens and okra. Twenty-five dollars." Before the man can get out his cash, she has begun to walk away.

They only take cash here; you hope you brought enough, as you look through your wallet. Thankfully, you brought a couple of twenty-dollar bills with you. Sipping the last of your beer, you lackadaisically walk to the end of the bar where you wait to pay your tab. The waitress takes her time getting to you; she's been busy cleaning the table in the corner for the umpteenth time today.

"Twenty-three dollars." Leaning her arm on the bar, her patience wears thin as she waits for you to hand over the money. "Thanks dear," the waitress says when you put a few extra bucks in the tip jar. Then she reminds you, "Don't forget to check out our gift shop."

Turning around, you walk through the bar to a side room filled with an assortment of hats and magnets featuring Eischen's Bar or Oklahoma logos as well as the occasional rubber chicken.

The "from the farm" ambiance is echoed throughout the building. You're reminded not to bring open beer bottles outside this establishment at every door with a sign. You think it's sad that they have to have signs. You challenge a friend to a shooting' game dedicated to hunting deer and bears as the jukebox plays "Simple Man."

Before leaving, take one last look around the bar and see a trophy case filled with memorabilia about the Eischen family and the bar. Old photographs and shopping buggies tell the bar's proud story.

Walking toward the door, you see a painting of a wild-looking chicken and pause to look closely at the funny face. A friend says, "When I die, I want to come here." Pushing open the green door, you squint, allowing your eyes to acclimate to the sun once again.

After getting to your car, you're still able to smell the chicken on your fingers. Immediately, you know, you'll be back. Bring some friends and family along on your next visit, but prepare them for the experience. Let them know there won't be prepackaged food. There's no low-fat, low-carb, or low-cal here. Miller Lite is the best you'll find. It's a simple place for a simple man. If you go in looking for anything more than the best fried chicken in Oklahoma you'll be disappointed.

III. Shared & Sharing: Experiencing Oklahoma & the Centennial

The first Van's Pig Stand, Wewoka, OK. Founder Leroy "Van" Vandegrift is 2nd from right. Photo courtesy of Van's Pig Stands Shawnee, Inc

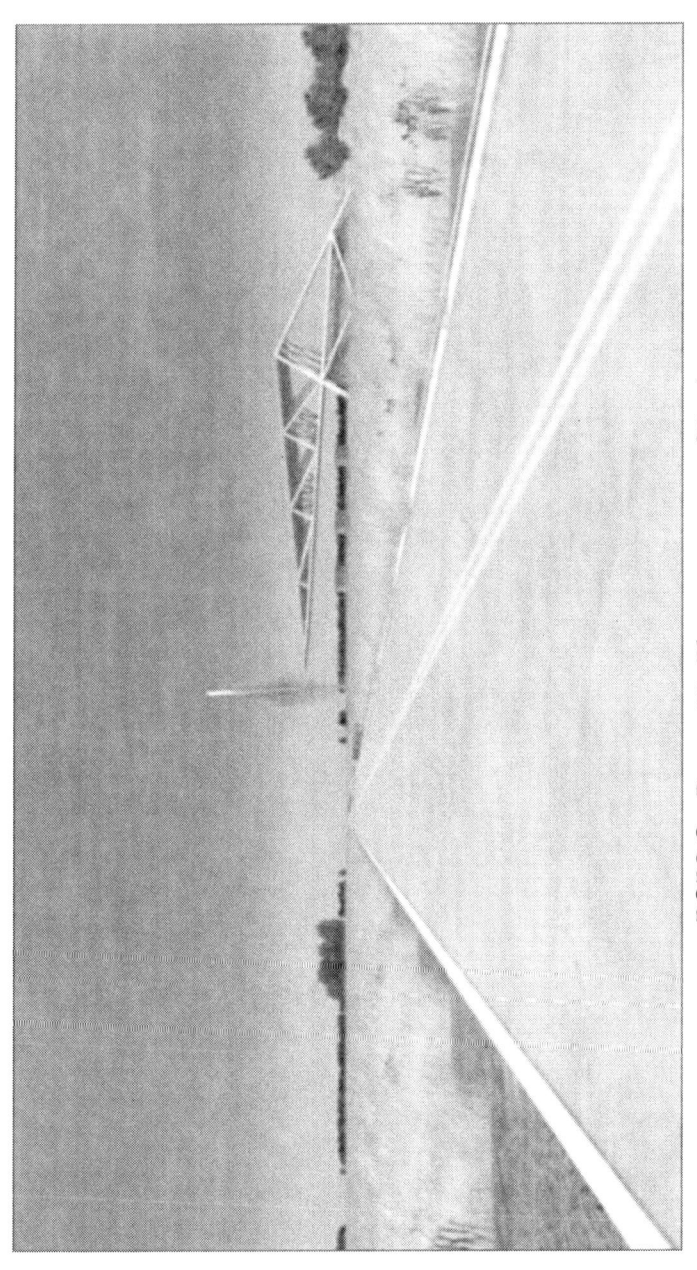

10. Sweet Treats & Good Eats

POPS On Route 66. Photo courtesy of Pop's

III. Shared & Sharing: Experiencing Oklahoma & the Centennial

Photos by Sarah Buchanan

11. Caught Up in Celebration: Remembering the Oklahoma Centennial Parade
By Gage Jeter

I pulled off my red and white shako, wiped the sweat from my forehead, and took in a deep breath of fresh Oklahoma air. It was all over quickly. I had just taken part in one of the biggest celebrations surrounding our state's centennial. The experience of marching in the Oklahoma Centennial Parade with the Pride of Oklahoma marching band has been tattooed in my memory so I can share it with my children, grandchildren, and great-grandchildren. Taking part in this event is something I will be proud of forever.

The Pride was selected along with several other college and high school marching bands to participate in the parade. Held in downtown Oklahoma City, the parade was expected to draw in hundreds of thousands of people, and it did. I saw them as I marched by playing our state song. I saw my mom, my grandparents, my great-grandparents. Coming from a long line of Oklahomans – natives of the Choctaw tribe, I could clearly see my past in all of the faces that lined the side of the streets. These people came out to celebrate!

However, celebration was the last thing on my mind when my alarm clock buzzed at 8 a.m. the morning of the parade. I spent my entire Saturday participating in homecoming events and then played for four hours at the football game Saturday night, all I really wanted to do was get some sleep. Our band director, Mr. Britt, who planned the itinerary for Sunday, had other ideas. We left Norman in six Red

Carpet charter buses at ten o'clock and drove to downtown Oklahoma City. When we arrived, I saw the crowd of people already beginning to form, even though the parade would not start for hours.

We arrived early. Very early. Warming up in sectionals took less than 30 minutes, so we restlessly meandered around the blocked off streets. Looking around, all I saw were yards overgrown with weeds, worn sidewalks, even homeless people sleeping under a nearby overpass. What could there possibly be to celebrate here? After 100 years, is this all our state had to offer?

I did not want to be there. I was tired, the sun was hitting me right in the face, and there was no shade to speak of. I wanted to crawl into my bed and sleep for hours, but instead I sat down on a hard curb and complained with others. "Take us home!" was our battle cry.

But my attitude soon changed. With almost three hours of downtime, I thought about my situation. I was a member of the Pride of Oklahoma. For the third year, I was selected to be in the most prestigious spirit group on the campus of the University of Oklahoma. Many people would have loved to have been in my shoes, yet there I was – complaining, whining, groaning.

I thought more about what this event really meant – to me and to other Oklahomans. I saw the huge balloon animals and floats begin to fill with air: our state animal, the buffalo, an Oklahoma balloon with the word "Celebrate" written across it, an Indian headdress with colorful feathers and dancers trailing the float. Looking back to the weeds and damaged sidewalks, I knew every state in the country had a few cracks. The homeless who had been sleeping under

11. Caught Up in Celebration

the overpass came out of the shadows. They meandered toward the crowd. Just like the thousands already present, they too wanted to take part in this event celebrating their state.

This was Oklahoma. These were my fellow Oklahomans. With a changed mindset and proud to be a life-long citizen of this remarkable state, I was now ready to celebrate, too.

Time passed more quickly when I began to see the beauty in this event. The whistle blew sooner than I thought, so we lined up in parade formation, and we were ready to go. Even though we were the 25th entry in the parade, I could already hear the cheers and clapping from the crowd ahead. We led the procession of bands, so we would be the first instrumental group the crowd saw and heard. We kept our musical selections simple: the OU fight song, "Boomer Sooner," as well as our state song, "Oklahoma!" With the first drum cadence 'go-go' and "Boomer," we were off. The crowd immediately erupted in cheers and applause. For many the Pride seemed to be the highlight of the parade.

Marching in the middle of downtown Oklahoma City, the noise and people were a blur, yet somehow the faces were so clear and distinct. The atmosphere of the parade was something I'd never experienced before. A smile was present on the face of every individual. When "Boomer Sooner" would end, the crowd would yell as if they were in Oklahoma Memorial Stadium watching the Sooners score a touchdown.

As we continued to march through the streets of Oklahoma City, we came to an area surrounded by parking garages. Heading down E K Gaylord Boulevard, I heard the volume increase and rise with the crisp autumn air. People filled and literally hung out of all levels of the surrounding parking garages, and I heard their voices above all the rest. I looked up five stories in the air and saw hundreds of people waving, clapping, and cheering while we played the state song. Being the center of this celebration of statehood became real to me at that moment.

I forgot about the sweat dripping down my neck and back. My feet weren't tired from marching 15 blocks. I was simply having a good time. The parade was soon over. The crowd thinned out gradually until the sidewalks lining the streets were near empty. I walked to our buses, took off my uniform, and allowed the wind to cool my body.

Pulling away from downtown, I looked out the window and watched. I couldn't take my eyes off the beauty of Oklahoma City. The Survivor Tree that reminds us of past events and our constant hope for the future. The Oklahoma River flowing underneath Interstate-35. The colorful murals proudly announcing "Celebrate Oklahoma!" Back on I-35, I watched until the skyline of downtown Oklahoma City faded away. Then I reflected. The vivid memories of marching in the Oklahoma Centennial Parade will never fade away. And if they do, well, I can always drive back to downtown and find them again.

Reprise! Statehood Parade in Guthrie, OK & Macy's Thanksgiving Day Parade, New York

Several weeks later, we were on the road again, this time to march in the Statehood Day Parade in Guthrie, Oklahoma. While the historic district's historical environment was much different than Oklahoma City, the emotional atmosphere was similar. Again, thousands of my fellow Oklahomans

11. Caught Up in Celebration

filled the streets of downtown Guthrie, the original capital. We sang Oklahoma! as we marched, and it was inspiring to hear the crowd sing along with us in unison. Seeing clashes of crimson and orange, I knew we weren't just celebrating statehood, but also the presence of two very different universities, OU and OSU. The parade was a memorable, enjoyable experience; however what most of us had on our minds was our next upcoming destination: New York City.

The following Monday the Pride boarded seven airplanes and flew to New York to march in the Macy's Thanksgiving Day Parade. After several flights delays, we arrived in New Jersey during the wee hours of the morning. Fatigue and exhaustion were put to the side with the excitement of being in the Big Apple.

The sole representative of the state of Oklahoma, the Pride was able embody the sprit of our great state and showcase our talent for millions of viewers, both live and on television. Not only did we march in the parade, but we were fortunate enough to have two full days to sightsee in New York. There was much to see and do, but the trip ended too quickly, and soon we were back home in Oklahoma Memorial Stadium cheering the Sooners on to a victory over Oklahoma State.

These significant celebrations I was able to be a part of have had a great impact on me. I consider myself blessed and have a greater appreciation for not only our state, but our country as well. Whether it was traveling 30 minutes to Oklahoma City, or taking a four-hour flight to New York, I was caught up in a wonderful time, the celebration of years and years of accomplishments and achievements.

The author, Gage Jeter, in New York, with The Pride

12. This is Oklahoma Football...
By Sarah Evans

The shout from the announcer, "It's football time in Oklahoma!" sends the crowd into a frenzy. This is what we wait months for, passing the time with basketball, baseball, recruitment news and all the other "sports" ESPN likes to put on during the off-season. Canada has hockey, and Boston and New York have baseball, but Oklahoma has football and is obsessed with it. People know better than to plan silly things like weddings or family reunions on a Saturday in the fall. They know no one will be there unless there is a TV that definitely gets the channel or if there is a bye-week. This fact is checked and rechecked and probably even verified with the satellite company before anyone reluctantly agrees to go.

My father and I are among these crazed people. We have had season tickets since 2003 and have only missed one home game in that whole time. We were one of the lucky few who got on the "List" after the 1999 season when things finally began to look better again for the team. I attended my first game in 2000 after Dad was lucky enough to get some tickets from his work. We watched Josh Heupel lead the Sooners to a huge win over the University of Texas El Paso that September. We would get single-game tickets off and on and attend whichever games we could until "The Letter" finally came my junior year of high school. The university was finally adding extra seating in the stadium and we would be given seats in the new upper-deck section on the east side, if we were interested. Needless to say, we were overjoyed. That year, my dad and I became two of "those fans,"

III. Shared & Sharing: Experiencing Oklahoma & the Centennial

the ones that rearrange their entire lives to fit in with football season and enjoy every minute of it.

This situation was not the case when I was growing up. The Sooners had a long stretch of bad luck starting in the late 80's with the "difficulties" Coach Barry Switzer had with his players. Some of the players went to jail, and Switzer resigned in 1989 starting a downward spiral worsened by years of poor recruitment and coaching. In the 1990s, tickets to the OU games were easy to come by, and no one wanted them. The name Gary Gibbs and Howard Schnellenberger are considered best forgotten by Sooner fans. Those were the years when we could not beat Texas or OSU and Sooner football games were rarely watched in our house. Dad would instead watch the playbacks of the old OU games and I grew up sheltered from the horror of the 90's, watching the likes of the Selmon brothers and Joe Washington break NCAA records left and right. I did not watch my first live game until 1998 when OU had hired a new head coach and his brother for a defensive coordinator. He was supposed to be pretty good so we bought the programming package from Dish Network that had the channel that was carrying the game. We watched a young team barely get beat by Texas A&M and thought that maybe things were turning around.

I now realize that being a Sooner fan was something instilled in me from an early age. "Boomer Sooner" and an inexplicable hatred for Texas and most anything that wore orange was drilled into my brain. Bud Wilkinson and Barry Switzer were THE coaches and I was able to easily list off the years in which the national championships were won and the names of all the Heisman Trophy winners. The first Halloween I went out trick-or-treating, I was an OU cheerleader complete with pompoms. As far back as I can remember I have always had something crimson and cream to wear and been able to clearly explain to OSU fans just how they could never be better than us. "How many National Championships does your team have? None? See, we ARE better!"

These days, Dad and I always go to the games, as my sister and mother do not really understand how football could be so appealing. Our own particular obsession usually begins each April and lasts until January. Schedules are memorized the minute they are finalized and pocket-sized rosters are printed out in the spring after the Red and White game. Then the wait begins for the large manila envelope that holds the tickets. Panic begins to set in if the package has not arrived by mid-August and frantic phone calls are made to the Athletic Ticket Office. When the tickets arrive, my dad and I will wait until we are both present to open the envelope to look at the new tickets. "Ah, they've changed the foil color again this year for the elevators." This worries my father. He sighs, "I TOLD them I have a letter saying my feet are bad and that my doctor says I can't POSSIBLY walk all the way up those ramps. The girl I talked to said they kept that sort of thing on file and that I wouldn't have to send it in again…I think." We both laugh at this and realize that it means yet another call to the ticket office, verifying that yes, we still can ride the elevators up to the upper deck.

Late August and early September finally arrive. We always leave our house at least an hour and a half before the game starts and head down Highway 9 into Norman with hundreds of other fans. We fall

III. Shared & Sharing: Experiencing Oklahoma & the Centennial

into line in our car, complete with OU auto emblem, and make the thirty-minute drive into Norman. Dad and I discuss the game ahead and the season so far as Al Eschbach and Jim Traber argue on the radio over who has the best teams in the country and whether or not OU will be in the title chase this year. We always park somewhere around Reeves Park and walk to the stadium in order to keep from paying to park. Something has always unnerved me about drunken college boys fitting hundreds of cars into incredibly small front yards, promising an easy exit and taking twenty bucks for their trouble. Dad and I only did that once, when we were running extremely late. Depending on how early the game is, how cold it is or who we are playing, the walk to the stadium is either noisy and rambunctious or far too calm and quiet.

The walk to Bedlam this year was quiet. Coming off a stunning loss to Tech and feeling cold and not all cocky, no one was hooting and hollering while waiting in line. "They're all nervous," my dad said laughing. "Heck, I know I am. It's not like it's some 'chump' game—this is for the Big XII." This made me think about the year college football fans have had. Parity was rampant. Schools like South Florida and Boston College were ranked far higher than anyone in the preseason would have dreamed and others like Michigan lose to a previously unheard of Appalachian State. Back in September, everyone knew OU was headed to the BCS Championship and that finally the press box on the west side of the field would be balanced with four years of national championship wins on one side and four on the other. Dreams were had that Sam Bradford would be the first ever freshman to win the Heisman Trophy.

12. This is Oklahoma Football...

The Miami game was the best football game I have ever been to. The crowd was fired up the game and we felt a sense of pride every time there was a delay of game penalty called or a timeout taken. It was the first time I ever felt Memorial Stadium shake because the crowd was so loud and it was amazing. It was said that Miami would be the best team that we would play this year and that if we could get past them with a win, we were shoe-ins for the Sears Trophy. After the game, Miami fans wished us luck, told us to really beat LSU because "They suck you know. They are just about the worst fans ever," and said to enjoy the national championship because it was ours.

The world stopped spinning for a minute when Colorado kicked a field goal as the last seconds of the game clock ticked away and all hopes of a perfect season flew out the window. My dad and I were probably among millions of Sooner faithful who sat in front of their TV sets, jaws on the floor, wondering how that could have just happened. I was the first to speak as we watched the Colorado fans tear down goal posts. "They had time outs. Why, for the love of god, did Stoops not call a time out or something? Colorado...we just lost to Colorado." "I...can't believe it either and I just watched it." "How far will we drop do you think, Dad?" "Does it really even matter? There's no way we're playing for it now. It's done and the best we can hope for is beating Texas. God, we need to beat Texas."

My dad was wrong for awhile. After a few more wins we were finally back up where we "should be" in the polls and teams like South Florida had been exposed. The Top 25 started to look less like the end of the world was drawing near and more like those of the past. All we needed was for a few teams to lose and then we would be back on top again and it would be like Colorado never happened. We managed to squeak by Texas in the Red River Shootout and break a losing streak that lasted far too long. Missouri and Iowa State were two close games that were won thanks to "Sooner Magic". A&M and Baylor were the blowouts they were expected to be. The halftime show for both featured the Pride dancing to Michael Jackson's "Thriller". I never thought that I would see the day that our band would make the precision marching of A&M look boring.

Then came Tech and everything changed again. We lost by a touchdown and four players left the game with injuries. Bradford looked so confused on the sidelines after his concussion. Doll-eyed and slack jawed, my dad commented that he "looked like an OSU fan." DeMarco Murray was injured on the last play of the game and two other players would go out with injuries. Could things get much worse? Bedlam loomed and the certainty of victory was questioned. Sure it is a home game this year but with Bradford potentially out and so many others in question, would Dad and I have to sit through our third home game loss and to OSU no less?

Luckily, we did not have to see our third home loss. OU scored early and often and Cowboys fans started leaving in the middle of the third quarter.

"Be a man and go for it Gundy!" was heard often towards the end of the game. Dad and I had an OSU fan sitting behind us who was quite friendly and told us all about their players and injuries. With that win, OU had clinched the Big Twelve South title again and was headed to play the winner of the Kansas-Missouri game in San Antonio.

12. This is Oklahoma Football. . .

December 1st was not only the day of the Big Twelve Championship but was also my parent's twenty-eighth wedding anniversary. They made sure to celebrate the day before so they could spend the evening at home watching the game. Dad was confident that we would not only win, but win big. I had my doubts. Missouri was ranked top in the nation and it is always difficult to beat a team twice in one year. We all began to get worried when the first quarter ended without a score. The defense was dominating but would the offense be able to do anything? The game was already ugly and penalty flags seemed to fly with almost every snap. Just seconds into the second quarter Chris Brown ran in a touchdown and we were finally ahead. The game just got better from there with amazing goal line stands that kept Missouri from scoring. Chase Daniel began to self-destruct early on and we watched and laughed as he attempted to pick fights with defensive players about twice his size. "We've just cost another quarterback the Heisman. Ain't it beautiful?" Dad asked laughing. In all, it was the perfect finish to Big Twelve play; the team finally managed to finish strong and played a wonderful game.

During the game it became evident that not only were we costing Missouri the National Championship, but we were also completely messing up the BCS; Dad and I thoroughly enjoyed that. The commentators during the game began to offer suggestions on who would be playing in New Orleans. Calls for a playoff system were heard around the nation as at least four teams had a good reason to play in the title game, OU being one of them. It would all depend on where we were ranked the next day.

III. Shared & Sharing: Experiencing Oklahoma & the Centennial

The BCS rankings came out on Sunday with Ohio State and LSU ranked one and two respectively. Oklahoma finished out the season eleven and two and ranked fourth in the nation. Not bad for a team that lost to two unranked teams during the regular season. The team will travel to Arizona in January to play the West Virginia Mountaineers in the Fiesta Bowl.

Author Sarah Evans & her best football buddy, her Dad.

Epilogue: Are You Doing Fine, Oklahoma? An Assessment at 100 Years
By Steven Eiler

Where the wind comes sweeping down the plain, it breathes life into a wildfire. When the wind comes right behind the rain, it meets with a cloud to give birth to a tornado. Oklahoma, you have teemed with these forces since long before humans set foot here. They are destructive, but they are also cleansing and renewing. They maintain a balance in the land so that life is sustained. Can the same be said of the forces wrought here by humans?

Every wave of settlers that has crashed against your sandy soil has brought with it innovation and destruction as well as a new generation who calls itself "native." As civilization has built its own clocks and then tried to outrun them, so have the waves come at a faster pace – some in a great upheaval and others overtaking them from the pull of momentum. It has not been so long that our maps have been drawn with the shape of a rusted cleaver in the middle. That pot with a cannonball shot through the bottom has only been called "Oklahoma" for a brief 100 years. It has not been a tumultuous century–most of the noisiest action took place before 1907– but it at least has been dynamic.

You have been a stopping place for outlaws and lawmakers, socialists and capitalists, European folks, African folks, plenty of other immigrants, and plenty of indigenous folks both self-settled and forcefully persuaded to uproot and move here.

We know we belong to the land, or at least we used to. We discovered oil within your soil, and we will not stop drilling till we've bled you dry. We have

Epilogue: Are You Doing Fine, Oklahoma?

given birth to a handful of luminaries and you have nurtured them, some burning dimly and others burning bright enough to light a generously sized living room in one of your thousands of suburban houses. You have allowed the growth of two semi-metropolitan hubs. You have been patient; you have not picked at the scabs but for the occasional scratch of a tornado or minor earthquake. The wounds will heal, don't you worry.

We citizens who walk upon your ground are a healing people. Our backs bear the scars of the scourge of slavery. Kids are still coughing up dust that their grandparents swallowed when we dug into your own back and you sloughed off your skin. Many of us are just now rebuilding a sense of tribal identity after centuries of learning were scraped clean by decades of education.

And what have you taught us? That the rain doesn't follow the plow; it comes when it pleases. That the ground will only do our work when we allow it time to rest. And what have we taught each other? You give what you can and you take what you're given. You leave what you lose and you never look back.

You have lost your land, your innocence, your wildlife. Your open spaces have been carved up by interstate highways and populated by lives far wilder than any of those we have tried to decimate. Our neighbors have adapted, not knowing how to fight back. Scissortail Flycatchers have taken to our chain-link fences and electric wires, and bison have taken to our prairie preserves, our museums, mythologies, and refrigerator magnets.

But we are a kind, gentle people – strong and healthy despite our heritage. We were raised with

Southern charm and Western ambition—the deaf children of Southern prejudice and Western expansion, the grandchildren of blind pride. Our closet doors are closed, but the skeletons beneath our skin will carry us far enough.

The top that Teddy Roosevelt set spinning when he dropped his pen to paper that November 16th has run into a few bumps, and it has long been wobbling and slowing down. Who among us will be able to start it up again? Oklahoma, okay... we've made it this far, but what about the future?

Contributors

Elisabeth Brown recently graduated from the University of Oklahoma with a degree in English writing and a minor in criminology. Her future plans include attending the University of Oklahoma College of Law in August 2008 and working for a local law firm. Elisabeth enjoys traveling, reading, spending time with family in Oklahoma and playing racquetball. She hopes to work as a sports agent after graduating.

Sarah Buchanan is now graduated from OU with a degree in English writing and Native American literature. From Tulsa, she is a member of the Cherokee tribe. She now has a writing career in Chicago.

Katrina Colbert is 21 and was born in Oklahoma City but raised in Ardmore. Her major is language arts education. She is a senior and will graduate in Dec. 2008

Andrew Edgren is an English writing junior from Texas, who writes in creative nonfiction and autobiographical genres. He has traveled extensively in his lifetime.

Steven Eiler is the son of a dentist and former elementary school art teacher. He is a music graduate, born in Illinois, who has spent most of his days in the great state of Oklahoma.

Lunden England is a senior at OU studying film and video studies as well as English. He plans to go to graduate school to study screenwriting. He is from Seiling and a proud member of the England clan.

Sarah Evans lives in Newalla, which is just outside of Oklahoma City. She is an English writing senior who will graduate in December 2008. Her favorite author is Gene Shepher and she enjoys watching movies and discovering new music.

Catherine L. Hobbs was born and raised in Oklahoma. She is on the faculty of the University of Oklahoma English Department.

Gage Jeter is a senior Language Arts Education major at the University of Oklahoma. He was born and raised in Tishomingo and is proud to be a part of this project. He has been active in the Pride of Oklahoma marching band for the past three years and was a member of the 2005-2006 President's Leadership Class. After graduating in December 2008, he plans to complete his student teaching in the Norman area and attend law school. His hobbies include swimming, spending time with friends, cooking, and reading for pleasure.

Born and raised in Jenks, America, Alisha Kirk is a proud Oklahoman. Graduating from the University of Oklahoma, she will be teaching English wherever life takes her. She loves to travel, read, and learn about new cultures and hopes to travel the world.

Contributors

Danielle Patricia Ann Knight (Cover Photographer) is a long-time resident of Norman, Oklahoma. Currently working towards her bachelor's degree in Fine Arts at OU, she hopes to some day become an art teacher. Danielle also has a strong interest in photojournalism and has shot for both the Oklahoma Daily and the Sooner Yearbook.

Sydney Teel is an English writing graduate of the University of Oklahoma. She grew up in Sapulpa. This fall, she enters the graduate program in English at her alma mater.

Christopher Turner, born in Lawton and a lifelong Oklahoman, graduated in May 2008 with a Bachelor of Arts degree with an English major and Spanish minor. He now works as a bilingual teacher in Dallas.

Made in the USA